Resistance to Change

A Guide to Harnessing Its Positive Power

Thomas R. Harvey and Elizabeth A. Broyles

ROWMAN & LITTLEFIELD EDUCATION
A division of
ROWMAN & LITTLEFIELD PUBLISHERS, INC.
Lanham • New York • Toronto • Plymouth, UK

Published by Rowman & Littlefield Education
A division of Rowman & Littlefield Publishers, Inc.
A wholly owned subsidary of
The Rowman & Littlefield Publishing Group, Inc.
4501 Forbes Boulevard, Suite 200, Lanham, Maryland 20706
http://www.rowmaneducation.com

Estover Road, Plymouth PL6 7PY, United Kingdom

British Library Cataloguing in Publication Information Available

Library of Congress Cataloging-in-Publication Data

Harvey, Thomas R.
  Resistance to change : a guide to harnessing its positive power / Thomas R. Harvey and Elizabeth A. Broyles.
     p. cm.
  Includes bibliographical references.
  ISBN 978-1-60709-214-8 (cloth : alk. paper) — ISBN 978-1-60709-215-5 (pbk. : alk. paper) — ISBN 978-1-60709-216-2 (electronic)
  1. Organizational change. 2. Organizational change—Management.
3. Leadership. I. Broyles, Elizabeth A., 1960– II. Title.
  HD58.8.H3755 2010
  658.4'06—dc22   2009053642

∞™ The paper used in this publication meets the minimum requirements of American National Standard for Information Sciences—Permanence of Paper for Printed Library Materials, ANSI/NISO Z39.48-1992.

Printed in the United States of America

To Mary F. Townsend, who has been
a lifelong friend and colleague.

Contents

List of Figures and Tables

FIGURES

TABLES

Acknowledgments

First of all, we wish to thank Michael Abraham for his kind donation of money to allow us the time to write this book. Without it, we would have taken far longer to compose this manuscript.

Secondly, we wish to acknowledge the doctoral students at the University of La Verne for their reviews, reactions, and dissertation research that went a long way in making this a quality work.

Finally, we wish to thank all those theorists that went before us upon whose shoulders we stand to view the issues of change in general and resistance in particular.

Part I

INTRODUCTION TO CHANGE RESISTANCE

CHAPTER 1

Resistance to Change

"I just won't do it" is the refrain for most of the changes that are proposed. Resistance. That is the bane of most change agents in organizations today. "If only people did not resist change and, instead, embraced change in its many forms, we would be a lot better off." Resistance. That is the heart of the change process. Resistance. That is what this book addresses.

Before we get into a discussion of the resistance process, let us pose a few change assertions.

CHANGE ISN'T RATIONAL

As much as we would like to believe that change is rational—that we just have to explain why change is for the better and the changee will do it—it isn't. Bennis, Benne, and Chin (1985) in their classic book on change describe these basic change strategies:

Power—coercive
Rational—empirical
Normative—re-educative

—short term

Power—coercive strategies are "push" strategies—for example, authoritative command ("I'm your boss, so do it!"), guilt, voting, and the like. These strategies are the fastest and most efficient in the short term, but they depend on your power to push them through. They are short-term strategies because they increase resistance and sow the seeds of your ultimate downfall.

S/T

power you to do this !

Rational—empirical strategies assume that people change through rational responses to new information. Research suggests, however, that rational approaches, though the most commonly used strategies, are actually the *least* effective (Hodgkinson, 1971). How many times have you seen wonderfully reasoned arguments and studies effect change? Seldom, if you are in the mainstream of management. Few human beings change solely because of new data or evidence. There are, indeed, settings in which rational approaches work, and individuals for whom they work, but those cases are the exceptions.

Smoking may be the most glaring example of the inefficacy of rational arguments in changing behavior. When the surgeon general first issued his reports on the negative impact of smoking on health, people generally agreed, but their habits changed very little. In fact, in the months following the early reports, the incidence of smoking actually *increased.* If smoking is any indicator, we would do well to turn to other, nonrational strategies to effect long-term change.

The third category, *normative—re-educative* change strategies, links a change to people's needs and drives. These are the strategies that try to identify the payoff for the changee. They have much in common with positive reinforcement strategies in psychology. The advantage of these approaches is that they have the most long-range impact. Their disadvantage is that they take the most effort and time to perform.

It is in this last category that the real change agent begins by carefully analyzing resistance and then figuring out the personal needs and drives that will work as antidotes to the resistance factors. As we've said, change isn't rational.

In fact, Pfeffer and Lammerding (1981) talk about three conditions that allow rationality to work:

1. clear, unambiguous goals
2. no conflict over priorities
3. plentiful resources.

The absence of just one of these conditions undercuts rationality. Just think of your organization. Do you have clear, unambiguous goals? No, in these tempestuous times, goals are always changing and new ones are being added constantly. Do you have conflict over priorities? Probably. It is a rare organization that does not have a conflict over priorities. Do you have plentiful resources? Hardly. In this resource-scarce world we live in, we never have enough resources. We most probably lack all three of these conditions, and we wonder why rationality doesn't work. Change is anything but rational.

COERCIVE CHANGE DOESN'T WORK

*only with Safety
fears*

Legislators try to mandate change, and it doesn't work. Authoritative managers try to command that change will take place, and it doesn't. No matter how appealing coercive change appears in terms of time and ease, it just does not work—at least in most organizations. When safety is an issue, then command decisions are appropriate. But, otherwise, coercion doesn't work.

Hold up your hand. Have someone push on it. What do you do? You push back. To resist force is a natural biological reflex. Coercion increases resistance. If you are strong enough, you can overcome resistance, but do not be mistaken about the outcome. The resistance does not dissolve; it merely goes underground—and that is where it is most dangerous. There is a wonderful old saying about resistance that is driven underground: "People have an infinite capacity to wait to get even."

Resistance that has been overpowered and driven underground will reappear at some other time or place when it is least expected. Some apparently innocuous issue will generate significant resistance, and you will wonder why. The real source, of course, is not this new issue but, rather, an older issue that has been festering for a month or a year or three years. The underground resistance you have created in the past will always bear fruit eventually. Coercive strategies for change increase the level of generalized resistance and thus decrease the probability of successful long-term change.

RESISTANCE TO CHANGE IS SANE   *Thus it makes sense!*

Yes. We said resistance to change is sane. In fact, it is the natural condition of things. It is unnatural not to resist changes. If someone proposes a change to you that will cost you more time or more money or increased burdens or more headaches, and you say, "Oh boy, when do I start?" you're insane. Insanity is defined as doing something against your best interests. If someone presents you with a change that doesn't reward you in some way, you shouldn't go along with it. It's up to the change agent to figure what's in it for you.

I did some research years ago on situations where persons go along with changes for which they have no apparent rewards—at least in the broad sense of that term (Harvey, 2001). In about 10 percent of the cases people went along with the changes because they were "yes-men." Whatever came up in their organizations they said "yes" to. They were unthinking "go along to get along" people. This is not change but complacency; and if you have an organization filled with "yes-men," you are in great trouble.

In about 35 percent of the circumstances, people went along with the changes because they knew it didn't matter. It was merely cosmetic change. It was like rearranging the deck chairs on the *Titanic*. People didn't resist because they knew the changes didn't matter. It was just another organizational chart redrawing.

In about 55 percent of the occasions, people said "yes" and then went out in the parking lot and began their sabotage of the ideas. People said "yes" but really meant "no." They just couldn't say it to your face. And it is hard to fight parking lot resistance. People can hide behind rocks and trees and cars and take potshots at you. This is the more prevalent of the three situations and the hardest to combat!

I do a little experiment with buttermilk in which I take somebody from the audience who loves to drink buttermilk and have him or her convince someone who hates to drink buttermilk to drink it. Inevitably, the lover talks about how nutritious buttermilk is and all the benefits it provides. The hater just sits there and thinks how nauseous the smell of buttermilk is. The lover never asks questions or provides the hater with any reasons to drink the buttermilk. He simply assumes that change is rational and, given enough evidence, the hater will change. Instead, the hater resists because there is nothing in it for him to drink the buttermilk. After all, he is sane. Remember, it is up to the change agent to find something in it for the hater to drink it.

YOU MUST DIAGNOSE RESISTORS

In the evitable face of resistance to change, you must start by asking questions; you must start with a diagnosis of why people sanely resist

Celebrate resistance

change. Many practitioners see starting with questions as a weak strategy. But it is not. It is the strongest of strategies. There is an old truism in change that says, "The more the changer talks, the less change will occur. The more the changee talks, the more change occurs." You have to get the changees to talk about their reactions to the change, why they do not want to do it, what they would rather do, and the like. But no matter what, do not ask them questions in an accusatory manner. That only makes the changee defensive.

Celebrate resistance. Ask questions in a manner that the changee wants to talk and share his feelings. Ask why the change wouldn't work and why it would be a bad idea. Celebrate resistance. Not because you want to stop in the face of it. But only by understanding the shape of the resistance can you develop a strategy to overcome it. You need to assess the resistance factors and then figure out the antidotes for each.

need to understand the resistance!

REDUCE RESISTANCE

In classic force field analysis (Lewin, 1951) there are two sides to any change—forces that drive change and forces that resist change. These countervailing forces are in what is called a quasi stationary equilibrium. They are basically standing still. Therefore, to make the change happen you have to:

1. increase the driving forces, or
2. decrease the resisting forces

It is obvious that the best strategy is to turn a resistor into a driver. For instance, we haven't got the money to make *A* happen. But we find a way to make more money by doing *A*; therefore, we turn a resistor into a driver. But this is rare. So we are left with two options noted above. Which do we do?

Well, if you put more pressure on the drivers, you simply increase resistance. Think about pushing on an outstretched hand. The hand pushes back. Pushing strategies increase resistance. Whereas, if you choose the second of these strategies—decrease resistance—you begin the movement of change without any detrimental effects.

Behaviors = change possible

Reducing resistance is at the heart of the change process. If you diagnose why people resist, develop antidotes for these resistors, and then implement them, you are 90 percent on the way to change. Now it must be added that these antidotes must be stated in behavioral terms. There is another old change truism that goes: You can change behavior, but you cannot change attitudes.

If you want change to begin—at least in our lifetime—you must perform the antidotes in behavioral terms. You can try values clarifications and attitude shifts, but they won't work relative to changes. Attitudes were built over long periods of time. They are not about to change quickly. But behaviors we can change. So that is why antidotes must be in behavioral terms.

attitudes = no change

ORGANIZATION OF BOOK

These, then, are our change assertions. The following pages will be organized in the following fashion. First of all resistance must be put within a context of general change theory and resistance theory. Hence, the need for chapter 2. Then each of the sources of resistance will be explored in chapters 3–22. In addition to exploring the sources of resistance we will pose several questions you might use to assess whether or not they are present in your change effort. Finally, we will suggest antidotes—or strategies—to various sources. Because no one strategy works for all sources of resistance. We will then end with a proposed model of resistance-based change.

VOICE

Let us add a note about voice. We have purposely written in the first person to make the book more conversational. When we use "I," it may refer to Tom or Elizabeth. It doesn't matter to us nor should it to you. The point of the story is change and the conversation we are going to have about it.

CHAPTER 2

The Theory Behind Change

It is our purpose in this chapter to present a thumbnail sketch about the theory that undergirds change. We intend, in no way, to be exhaustive. We simply want to put the idea of resistance within a context of change theory.

BACKGROUND

Deliberations about the nature of change go back at least as far as the ancient Greek philosophers. And while this debate may still continue among our modern-day philosophers, even a cursory search of the word "change," in nearly any database, should convince just about all of us that the verdict is already in—*change is inevitable*. In fact, you've probably heard the argument that life in the twenty-first century means living in a near constant state of change.

Now that's not to say we don't still experience intervals of relative stability. Rather, it suggests these intervals are getting shorter while at the same time the frequency and duration of periods of change are actually increasing.

That means, at least in theory, that the debate is no longer about whether or not change happens; in point of fact we know it does. Rather, given this accelerating rate of change, the question really becomes "Is it possible to plan for and manage change?" We say the answer is unequivocally YES! We'd even go a step further and say that merely reacting to change is just not a viable option for any organization that wants to survive, let alone thrive in today's world.

That is why it is more important than ever for organizational leaders to know how to effectively plan for and manage change. That means a few things. First, it means believing that change can be managed. Second, it requires recognizing resistance as the key element of any change process; and third, it means acknowledging that change is all about possibility. The truth is that change really presents opportunities. The real task for change leaders today is helping others see the potential promise of change rather than fear change. After all, it is the fear of change that often leads to resistance. Knowing how to identify and plan for resistance is at the heart of a successful change process.

However, before we delve into a discussion about resistance, let's explore what we know about change theory. Then we'll be able to see resistance for the integral, natural, and valuable component of the change process that it is.

PLANNED VERSUS UNPLANNED CHANGE

Change. While change has been defined in a multitude of ways, at its core it simply means to move from one state of being to another, to become or do something different. Although all sorts of theories about change and change management abound, let's start with the most basic of questions, which is "Why is it that change happens?"

The answer is simple: change virtually always begins in response to some stimulus, whether internal or external, which motivates us to move from doing one thing to doing something else. While the specific motivations or circumstances that spur us on to change may vary, change rarely happens spontaneously. There is almost always some force, some impetus, that jump-starts the change process.

Sometimes change happens because we want to move toward something that we've decided is better, more desirable than what we currently have, or, conversely, because we want to move away from some thing or some practice we've come to view as bad.

I recently had an experience with this type of change motivation. You see, I've always been a big fan of four-wheel-drive vehicles because they get excellent traction in snowy, slippery conditions. However, they aren't so good when it comes to fuel economy. Some of the new hybrid cars have great results in the area of lowering gas consumption.

Now for me, at least in today's market of escalating gas prices, driving a really fuel-efficient car became more desirable than what I had been doing. So I made a change; I traded my higher-gas-consuming four-wheel-drive vehicle for a more fuel-efficient hybrid. That was the external stimulus for my change—my pocketbook.

And of course, there are always those times when change begins because someone has a new idea, a desire to do things in a different way, or a vision of what the future could look like. Such people see a discrepancy, a gap between what currently "is" and what "might be" and as a result they decide it's time to make a change. Whether or not that change is well received is another story, a story of resistance—which we'll get to momentarily.

Now it's absolutely important to recognize that although change almost surely happens in response to some stimulus, change itself can either be planned or it can be unplanned.

By its very nature, unplanned change is characteristically random and generally reactionary. Planned change, on the other hand, implies something much more deliberate, intentional. Think of it this way: planned versus unplanned change is the difference between being prepared for and responsive to change versus simply blowing in the wind, reacting willy-nilly to change as it heads your way.

The reality is that the viability of most organizations today generally rests in their ability to cope with and manage change. And of course, there's also the reality that change implemented in crisis mode typically fails.

What do we mean by planning for change? Well, we mean just that! We mean looking ahead at what's coming, considering possibilities, analyzing potential sources of resistance, strategizing, and then crafting and implementing your strategies. While we would agree that change is a dynamic, shifting animal, that doesn't mean you can't or shouldn't plan for it. After all, planning for change gives you a far better chance of being able to influence the course of the change. It can keep you from being pulled into misalignment, where your actions, your goals, and your vision just don't match.

Additionally, when you approach change in a willy-nilly fashion you are bound to end up with uneven, incomplete, haphazard results (Test, 1991). And then there is the reality that planning for change always aids in its successful adoption and long-term institutionalization. The bottom line is that planning for change equals a greater likelihood for its successful adoption and integration into "the way we do things around here."

PLANNED CHANGE AND OD

One last word regarding the benefits of planning for change: planned change and organizational development (OD) are two sides of the same coin; they are sister images. Both are about being proactive and making informed choices. In today's world, taking a proactive approach, which includes, nay requires, a clear process, is essential in successfully responding to change.

When you really think about it, OD is both a strategy and a process for achieving growth. In this case growth is really synonymous with learning, and learning is inextricably connected to change. You might even say that OD is growth through change and that learning equals change. In fact, Bennis, Benne, and Chin (1985) astutely suggested that organizational development is really planned learning.

If we take that thought just a step further, when we recognize the world as a changing and dynamic place, there is a clear need for continuous learning within our organizations. In fact, that is why so many organizations are moving down the path toward becoming "learning organizations." Learning organizations are those that are engaged in ongoing organizational development, and this OD, if it is to be successful, is dependent upon planning. And planning MUST address resistance!

Before we move on, a simple word of caution is worth including. Mintzberg and Huy (2003) sagely encourage us to pause and take a look at our apparent fascination, perhaps even obsession, with the idea that change is constant and unceasing. They suggest this sense of constant change is really a matter of perception. People *notice* the changes. But, as we've already pointed out, there are still periods of stability, and stability is good. After all, as Mintzberg and Huy (2003) suggest, change would have no real meaning without continuity, and because things do remain stable, at least from time to time, change must be managed with an eye toward stability. That means, yes, you guessed it, planning for change!

READINESS FOR CHANGE VERSUS STRATEGIZING FOR CHANGE

There has been much written about the idea of readiness for change. There are dozens of tools, designed for a variety of environments, from educational to nonprofit settings, to help you assess your organization's "readiness" for change.

We would suggest that assessing readiness for change is really a part of the analysis process that any effective change process must engage in if it hopes to be successful.

If you adequately and effectively assess your organization and find that it is ready to make a proposed change, well, hooray! In such a circumstance change tends to occur fairly easily; moving forward with the change is a natural next occurrence.

Change occurs naturally if you're ready. However, 85 percent of the time, when you decide to start implementing a change, particularly if you haven't done your homework, what you're likely to discover is that people AREN'T ready.

What is the natural response from people who don't feel ready to make a change? RESISTANCE. That is the nature of resistance. People aren't ready.

When you discover that people aren't ready for change, and you are likely to find at least a few, you are left with two basic options. You can do one of two things. You can give up. *Or* you can strategize about how to get people ready. Those are really your two choices. You can stop in the face of resistance, or you can start planning to address this resistance.

You have two basic options when you encounter resistance—give up or strategize. We propose strategizing.

There it is in a nutshell. If you want change to be successful—to become institutionalized—you must first conduct a thorough analysis, looking at everything from who will be affected by the change to where your potential sources of resistance may lie. Then you can actually begin to ascertain readiness for change and plan to help people become ready. Then and only then are you ready to begin implementing your change. And of course, if you want change to be successful, you have to plan for its institutionalization at the beginning, not the end.

Once you know where your resistance lies, you are ready—not to make the change, but to strategize, to craft strategies to address resistance in order to be ready to move forward. It is this strategizing about addressing resistance factors and decreasing resistors that is really the key to your successful change efforts.

TRANSFORMATIONAL CHANGE VERSUS TRANSACTIONAL CHANGE

Need transactional change for transformational to happen

While there may be a great deal of conversation occurring in the literature around the idea of transformational change, we would suggest that such discussion has a tendency to be a little misleading.

Transactional changes are incremental and they are most often adaptive in nature. Typically, transactional changes occur when some general feature or aspect of the organization changes, but the fundamental nature of the organization remains the same.

Let's take a simple example. Perhaps your school district decides to adopt a new electronic student report software program, one which you believe will assist teachers and administrative staff in more efficiently preparing and disseminating progress report cards. This is a transactional change. Why? You have not fundamentally changed the nature of your school district or transformed its structure, but you have implemented a change designed to improve performance.

While transactional changes may require some basic staff training and development, they can usually be implemented using current knowledge, practices, and skills. Heifetz and Linsky (2002), in their well-known book *Leadership on the Line*, refer to these types of changes as those that address technical problems.

Now, unlike transactional changes, transformational change is change that alters an organization (or a person) in more radical, profound ways. The nature of the organization is substantially changed; it is, yes, that's right—transformed. Such changes are more complex, and they typically require an organization to stretch, to extend beyond what it currently knows or does.

However, the most important thing to realize is that transformational change cannot occur in the absence of transactional, adaptive changes. It is through a series of these incremental changes that organizations can be led into real transformational change.

Perhaps one of the more profound illustrations of transformational change would be those changes that impact organizational culture. For example, changes in decision-making authority (deeply rooted in organizational culture) often require a significant transformation of organizational attitudes and behaviors.

Let's consider the following scenario. Throughout an organization's history, all decisions of import, including customer requests, have always been vetted through various layers of upper management. However, given an ever-increasing fluctuation in the market, it has become clear that decision-making authority must be afforded much closer to the front line, say, between the customer service staff and the customers themselves. That's a fairly radical shift. Such a major change of events can't occur overnight.

Can you imagine? Your boss walks into your office at the close of business and says, "Sarah, I know I've always been in charge of making all the final decisions about what accommodations we can make for customers, but starting tomorrow, I'm leaving that up to you. Good luck!" EGADS, you shriek!

However, what if instead your boss incrementally allowed you to assume control over one decision area at a time? Imagine the possibilities! Taking a transactional approach, taking smaller steps, ones that allow organizational members (at all levels) to adjust, to feel comfortable with and more confident in such a radical change, has the potential to transform not only a historic power structure, but the way in which the needs of organizational customers could be met.

We believe that in reality, all change is really composed of transactional changes. What does that mean? It means that when you implement a number of smaller changes that coalesce around similar change ideas, together these changes can become transformational.

The best way to achieve intentional transformational change is by engaging in thoughtful, planned, incremental transactional changes, changes that are tied to and guided by an organizational vision for change. Without this planning and vision, while you may still find yourself forced to make radical changes at some point in the future, you will likely find yourself at the mercy of the elements, and you may not end up where you'd ultimately like to be!

LEWIN'S THREE-STAGE CHANGE MODEL

According to Lewin (1951), considered by many to be the father of change theory, there are three primary phases or stages to the change

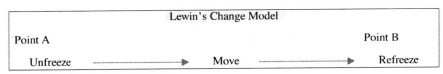

Lewin's Change Model

Point A   Point B

Unfreeze   ─────────────►   Move   ─────────────►   Refreeze

Figure 2.1. *Lewin's Change Model*

somewhere to go

process: *unfreezing* from point A, *moving* toward point B, and, finally, *refreezing* at point B.

It is the first phase of the change process, the unfreezing, that is essential for change to occur. After all, if you can't unfreeze, if you stay stuck in the spot you are currently in, how can you possibly move people in the direction of the change you'd like to make?

Lewin's force field analysis was designed to assist in the identification of drivers, those individuals or forces that favor a proposed change and can become a driving force behind the change, and restraining forces (resistors) representing those forces (individuals) that are likely to oppose or be against a given change (resistance). As we've already said, it is this resistance that provides the central challenge to implementing successful change.

Why is this so? In a typical force field analysis (as illustrated in figure 2.2), you have two forces: driving and restraining.

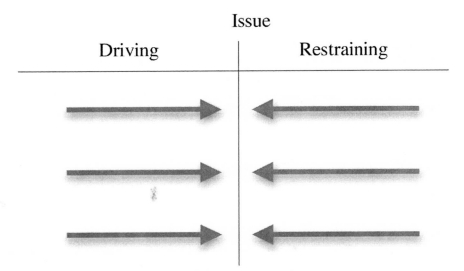

Issue

Driving   Restraining

Figure 2.2. *Force Field Analysis Issue: Driving/Restraining*

These forces are generally in a state of equilibrium; that is, things aren't changing. To create change, you can either increase the pressure of the driving forces OR you can decrease the resistors. The trouble is, when you increase the drivers, you concomitantly increase the resistors.

As we said before, push on someone's hand. The more pressure you apply, the more resistance you get. You may apply enough power to overcome the resistance, but you've not done away with it. You've merely driven it underground. As we mentioned earlier, we have an important principle of change about underground resistance: "People have an infinite capacity to wait to get even." Resistance driven underground builds up too much sabotage. That is why it is far better to deal with the forces that resist rather than the driving forces.

Identifying possible sources of resistance is only a first step, however. In order to get people to "unfreeze," to be even remotely interested in or willing to change, to move toward a new point B, three preconditions must be met: the right conditions of strain (stress, urgency); a sense of potency; and clear, adequate valence (Harvey, 2001; Frohman, 1970). Let's look at each of these in a bit more detail.

The first precondition to unfreezing is *stress* (or strain). Without stress, or urgency, people are hardly inclined to learn anything new or to do things differently. The trick is to exert enough stress to cause movement, without applying so much that you create a state of *distress*. This can't be emphasized enough. We tend to think about stress as bad, but stress or tension is really a good thing, in the right amount. Why? Because *stress leads to growth.*

When stress in an organization is too low, there is no motivation to change. In fact, comfort is really the enemy of change. However, when stress is too high, people can feel overwhelmed; they become incapable of coping with change. They shut down, hide under their desks, and become essentially immobilized.

There is a middle ground, however: EUSTRESS—that is, a state of healthy stress. It is just the right amount of pressure to promote curiosity or urgency and create a positive environment to grow or change. That is the first goal of the change leader—creating an environment, crafting the right strategies to generate the right level of stress to help people begin to move toward a particular new point B.

That brings us to the second precondition of unfreezing—*valence*. Valence simply means the degree of attractiveness that point B possesses—whether point B is a behavioral goal, an individual, an activity, a thing, or a place to be.

So you see, valence is related to the attractiveness of the change being proposed, the *new point B*. It is critical that the changee views point B as something positive, rather than merely experiencing point A as a state to get away from. This means the payoff for arriving at point B must be positive.

If point A is just something bad to get away from, you may move, but not very far, and you may not end up at point B at all, but rather at some point A[1], close to where you started. That is why payoff, the payoff for the changee (NOT the change agent), is so critical—payoff must be attractive enough to get people to jump over the fence of change, and it must be positive enough to encourage them to stay there (Harvey, 2001).

Potency is the third precondition necessary for unfreezing. People must not only be motivated to change, they must also believe they are capable. There's a saying that goes, "If you say you can, or if you say you can't, you are right." Change will occur only if the changee believes they have the potency, the ability to change. You can only change if you believe you can.

It is probably evident by now that the second phase of the change process—*movement*—is a function of not only having someplace to go but also a belief that you have the skills to get there. Once you have created sufficient stress or a desirable point B to head toward, and a sense of capability to make the change, movement can happen. In other words, once people become unfrozen, that is, motivated to change, they are ready to move. Remember, getting to this stage requires that the change agent acts strategically, planning and developing alternatives and strategies, in order for movement to happen.

MODELS OF CHANGE

Since the time Lewin first developed his three-phase change model, a whole host of models have been created to guide change agents through the process of planning for and implementing change.

Most, if not all, of the change models described in the literature or marketed to change leaders today fall into one of three basic categories:

- directive models
- collaborative models
- combination models

The *directive model* is really an authoritarian change model. In this type of model, change leaders act as the main controller of the process, making most of the decisions, telling people what to do and often how to do it. Directive models rely heavily on "push" strategies. Decisions are made by those at the top, those in positions of power, whereas the people required to do the actual work of implementation tend to have little if any input into the decisions that will affect them.

The directive model can be both an appropriate and effective choice when time is of the essence, that is, when rapid-fire decisions and quick changes must be made. However, beware the hidden pitfalls of using such a model, particularly if you rely on this type of approach for all your change efforts.

One of the greatest drawbacks of directive models and their typically coercive strategies is the amount of resistance they tend to generate. Oh, you might initially get employee compliance with the use of your heavy-handed tactics, but beware! People have a long memory and an enduring propensity to get even. Not only that, they will take their frustration and resistance underground, where you can't see its immediate effects, and then get ready for the sabotage to begin. It's only a matter of time before people revolt, whether passively or actively, when they are constantly pushed to change but rarely involved in the change decisions that affect them directly.

Of course there are also *collaborative* change models. The key monikers for models that fall into this category are *inclusion* and *collaboration*. The difference between this type of model and a more directive approach is the difference between creating the change "with" stakeholders versus doing the change "to" them. This is not to say that the rallying cry of the collaborative model is always "the more the merrier," or "y'all come," but rather that a conscious effort is made by change leaders to involve those stakeholders who will be affected by potential changes.

Bennis, Benne, and Chin (1985), well-known writers in the field of planned change, have suggested that collaborative models are really the sine qua non of effective planned change. And it's certainly true; there are many, many benefits to this type of change model.

For example, as a result of including more people, you are likely to generate much greater buy-in to your proposed change, and you may even reduce your implementation time as a result. Of course, you need to be strategic about whom you include, making sure you are inviting the right people to participate! That's another reason why doing your homework is so important. If you invite the wrong players or, worse yet, leave out the important ones, you're just as likely to shoot yourself in the foot as if you were to overuse directive models.

Like the directive models, there are also drawbacks to using the collaborative models. Perhaps one of their greatest challenges is their tendency to be very time intensive, as well as generally requiring more effort and energy than their directive counterparts. In addition, strictly collaborative change models undertaken without good leadership (and sometimes even with) can devolve into a state of seeming nondirection, waffling around the edges of uncontrollability. However, the long-term benefits, when properly implemented, can include decreased resistance and an increased probability that the change will be sustained over the long haul.

In an effort to take full advantage of the benefits of both models, while also minimizing their potential drawbacks, a few theorists have created change models that combine the finer points of each of the other two types. For example, Harvey's (2001) model of directive collaboration allows managers to shift between directive and collaborative strategies at key points during the change process. Such models have the potential to minimize misunderstandings, facilitate collaboration on key issues, and keep the change manager in control while concurrently promoting participation.

As we've seen, each category of change models has both advantages and disadvantages. It's important to also note that the plethora of change models available to choose from actually exist on a continuum, from highly collaborative to extremely coercive.

Whichever category you select from, whatever style and specific model you choose, it is critical for you to select the process best suited to your circumstances.

How will you know which model to choose? Ask yourself:

- What is the impetus, the reason, for this change?
- What is our current environment like, and what is it likely to be down the road?
- Who will be most/least affected by any changes?

- How much time do we have to implement the change?
- How important is trust as an issue?

The answers to questions like these can guide you in making your selection. Remember, whether you choose collaborative, directive, or some combination of the two, any model has the potential to either garner support or generate resistance, depending on the situation at hand. So do be sure to choose wisely.

CHANGE MODELS—MORE ALIKE THAN DIFFERENT

Up to now, we've allowed our discussion of the three main categories of change models to focus primarily on what makes these models different. We would be remiss if we did not also address the ways in which many change models tend to be similar.

First, most change models recognize change as a process, one which proceeds through a series of phases. Additionally, nearly all of the change models you are likely to encounter are built on Lewin's original three-phase model.

The primary difference between most change models really revolves around the number of steps various authors suggest occur within the different phases of change. That's not to imply that the change process is inherently linear, but rather that it proceeds in stages, or phases. Additionally, the activities within each phase may—and often do—overlap.

Perhaps some of the better known change models include Zaltman's (1977) ten-step problem-solving model; Lippitt, Langseth, and Mossop's (1985) seven-step approach; or Kotter's (1996) eight-step process. Others, such as Harvey's (2001) Checklist for Change, utilize a three-phased, twenty-step approach, while Jim Collins (2001), in *Good to Great*, relies on a visual model—a flywheel—to describe the change process.

While the number of "steps" in each phase of a change model may differ, most change models rely on a similar framework. In reality, although the names and labels may vary slightly, there seems to be general agreement that the change process moves through three basic phases:

analysis,
planning and strategizing,
and *implementation*.

Embedded in the most successful change models, and something we adamantly suggest is an absolutely essential ingredient for any change process, is the ongoing use of regular *evaluation.*

Throughout the change process leaders not only should, but really MUST engage in a practice of ongoing assessment, strategizing, and evaluation of the various elements of the change process. AND, because change is a process, this assessment, planning, evaluation, and adjusting is just as important during the implementation stage of the change process as it is during the early stages of the process.

Now we can't emphasize this next statement enough, but remember: *The primary goal of the change process is to successfully institutionalize the change.*

In fact, as Harvey's research (2001) points out, you *cannot* institutionalize change after the fact! You MUST plan for the long-term incorporation of a change long before you ever, ever move into the implementation stage. And ongoing evaluation is a key step in accomplishing this.

Two final thoughts about change models are worth mentioning here.

First, as we've said, all change models include a series of steps and the change process isn't necessarily linear—there is always some movement between the phases. Additionally, if you are wise you'll certainly make little adjustments here and there, as evaluation informs your next steps.

However, that does not in any way suggest that it's OK to skip steps. To that we would say NO, NO, and NO again. As Kotter (1996) wisely points out, skipping steps only creates an *illusion* of speed. In the end, skipping steps will cost you more time AND will seriously impair your chances of long-term adoption of the change—giving you a double whammy. So do be diligent about working the process.

That brings us to our last point, and that is this: Change is a process, and having a process or model to follow is essential if you'd like your change to have any chance at all of being successful. In fact, Fox (2003), in her research on leading with change principles, discovered that the process used to initiate change is actually as important as the change itself.

The truth of it all is that while each of the various change models possesses some of its own unique characteristics, they are not only similar in their reliance on some type of three-phased framework but also tend to draw upon similar change principles. In fact, to really understand resistance, it's important to understand some of these key principles of change. Our next section will do just that.

PRINCIPLES OF CHANGE

There are many ways to construct a list of the various principles of change. We have chosen what we believe are the top ten principles and those that are most pertinent to helping understand where resistance resides in the change process. They are described below.

1. Change Is More Likely to Occur in Environments Conducive To or Favorable for Change

We would suggest that one of the very first things any change leader should do is create an environment that is actually conducive to change. What do we mean? Think of it this way. Both innovation and change require a certain amount of risk taking, and with risk comes the inevitability of some failures. However, if experimentation is allowed to happen in the right setting, where there is an attitude of "it is OK to fail sometimes," just think of how much more we can learn through our attempts.

On the other hand, consider those work environments where no one is willing to try something new, take a risk, or even suggest a different way of doing things. What do you usually find in those situations? Typically there is some "Attila the Hun" waiting near the top of the food chain, ready to trounce any poor soul who shows even the slightest glimmer of interest in something different.

When you think of this sort of environment, where it's not OK to fail or even try new things, just how open to change do you suppose folks are likely to be? Not very! After all, who wants to be the recipient of that sort of fallout? People in such settings become conditioned to fear failure and the repercussions that go with it, and over time, a culture of fear eventually becomes entrenched.

However, there is light at the end of this particular tunnel. As change leaders, you may actually have the power to foster an environment where learning is valued, where errors that lead to learning can be accepted, and where risk taking can be encouraged, even rewarded.

Now this doesn't mean risk, risk, risk all of the time! No, not at all. What it does mean is creating structures that allow for "bounded risks," ones where some thought and strategizing have gone into the effort. That's very different than having no structure at all. Such structures can and should include employees at many organizational levels having the power to make decisions and take reasonable risks, without creating a sense of pure chaos. After all, while people don't typically tend to like chaos, they do like to learn, grow, and achieve.

When employees feel secure in their ability to take reasonable risks, their openness to change is increased. This is a good thing. In fact, environments that support change through bounded risk taking, particularly those that structure changes so employees experience more gains than risks, are environments that create a sense of success and potency. And that's the real payoff for creating an environment that supports change, because it really is true, success builds success!

The more thoughtful the risks you take are, the more successes you encounter, the more open you are to trying again.

2. Change Is Always Loss

This reality must never be overlooked—all change represents a loss for someone. Think about it. As we said at the beginning of this chapter, change essentially means moving from one way of being (or doing) to another, in other words to become or do something different. This means we must let go of what we were doing and pick up or integrate something new. And it isn't just that "we" are letting go of something, but that we are also asking, even expecting, others to do the same. That is where the real sense of loss comes into play.

Consider the following: If I ask you to let go of something, to get on my particular change bandwagon, I'm asking you to stop doing what you are currently doing. However, what if you really like doing things the way you do them? What if you created the current system I'm asking you to give up? What if you learned how to do what you do from someone you admired and respected? What if my asking you to change leaves you thinking that there is something wrong with the way you are doing things? What if you believe that you can truly be successful doing the same old things?

The answers to all of these questions are likely to be associated with a sense of loss: a loss of comfort in doing things a certain way; a loss of loyalty to those who taught us the old ways; a loss of prestige; a loss of confidence; even a loss of pride—just to name a few.

Why bring up the issue of loss? We bring it up because it is imperative for change agents to understand that because all change represents a sense of loss, all change generates both a natural sense of grief, AND, as a result, a level of resistance.

Consequently, if you want your change efforts to be successful, you need to recognize this perception of loss, provide opportunities to talk about it, and acknowledge it in the open. Believe it or not, it can even be extremely valuable to create opportunities to grieve this sense of loss WHILE looking forward with positive anticipation to new opportunities! Have a memorial service for that which you are about to leave and birth announcements for the upcoming change.

3. Change Inherently Involves Conflict

No matter how nice you are or how you dress up a particular change, any change will inherently involve some degree of conflict. Why? Well, for starters, let's consider the principle we just discussed. If all change involves loss (which it does), there is bound to be at least some degree of conflict between those who perceive that sense of loss and those who are pushing for or championing the change. Beyond this level of conflict are the inevitable conflicts and disagreements that emerge over how to move forward with a change: *What steps should be taken? In what order? How quickly or slowly? Who will be responsible for which aspects? Who should be impacted first? How many resources should be allocated or eliminated?* You can imagine the level of distress and conflict these decisions and discussions can generate!

Conflict! The word sends chills up many a spine. The truth is that most of us like to avoid conflict, often at almost any cost. The mere possibility of conflict tends to get our stomachs all tied up in knots. In fact, we've arguably become preconditioned to believe that conflict is in some way fundamentally bad. However, particularly when it comes to change, this notion is dead wrong. Why? First, because conflict in any change scenario simply isn't avoidable, nor should it be. Second, because conflict and stress are inextricably related.

Stress. It is not only an integral component of conflict, but it also reminds us of an earlier and very important premise: comfort is the enemy of change. Remember, in the absence of stress there is no change, merely the *illusion* of change. In reality, a certain amount of stress, tension, or conflict isn't bad; it's actually good. Why? Because *stress leads to growth.* Without a little healthy stress in the system—that is, *eustress*—there is little to no motivation to change.

The bottom line is this: while all change includes some element of conflict, and consequently stress, this is really a good thing, if, of course, it is approached appropriately, intelligently, and productively. After all, while the stress of conflict may (or may not) be productive for an organization's goal, it can still be uncomfortable. As a result, change leaders have to be prepared with conflict skills and strategies. This is particularly true now, living in a world *beyond the J curve.*

In a world beyond the J curve, there is the possibility for more conflict than ever before. Up until the mid-1900s, most would agree, we lived in a time of relative periods of stability, interspersed with occasional "spasms" of change. For the most part, there was adequate time to plan and act in relative ease within the organizational world. Time seemed to move more slowly. Changes came, but at a generally manageable pace.

But no more. Today's generations are living in a world where change is occurring at an ever accelerating, some would say even dizzying rate, interspersed with occasional "spasms" of stability. This escalation has resulted in forming most phenomena into a J curve, as shown in figure 2.3 (Harvey, Bearley, and Corkrum, 2002).

Let's look at just a few examples of how this phenomenon is playing out. Consider the exponential rate of change occurring in the areas of

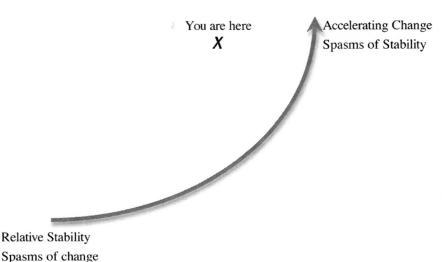

You are here
X

Accelerating Change
Spasms of Stability

Relative Stability
Spasms of change

Figure 2.3. *J Curve*

technology and information. While we won't claim that our numbers are *entirely* accurate—and of course by the time of this publication, they will have changed *again anyhow*—we provide the following to give you a flavor for just how rapidly things are changing.

- In 1984 there were approximately one thousand Internet devices in use. In 2008 the number grew to one billion (that's right, *billion*) and projections are that in 2010 that number will explode to thirty-five billion.
- In 2006, 2.7 billion Google searches were performed each month. The number for 2008: thirty-one billion per month.
- In 2008, it's been estimated that approximately four exabytes or EB (that's 4.0×10^{19}, or one *quintillion* for those of you not up on your computer technology terms) of unique information were generated.
- New information is reportedly now doubling at a rate of approximately every seventy-two hours. What does that mean for students starting their four-year college degree in 2008? It means that half of what they learn in their first year will be outdated by their third.
- According to a very clever, very popular video "Did You Know? 3.0," which you can view for yourself on YouTube, "We are preparing students for jobs that don't exist, using technologies that haven't been invented, in order to solve problems we don't even know are problems yet!"

Are you dizzy yet? As you can see, in the world beyond the J curve, change is endemic. What does that mean? It means that there is a lot of change in the air, and with that comes the propensity for things to bump into each other, create friction, and yes—conflict! Change and conflict are indeed intertwined. The wise change leader will keep this in mind, brush up on her conflict management skills, and embrace this reality with open arms.

4. In the Absence of Shared Ownership, Change Is Likely to Fail

There's an old, but very wise adage: "If they haven't bought it, they aren't going to keep it." What does that mean? It means that participation and collaboration are keys to successfully moving any change forward.

The more people are included in making decisions about what changes to make and how they should be made, the more likely they are going to be to feel a sense of ownership toward that change. This is particularly true when you include those most likely to be affected by a proposed change. In fact, Glaser (2005) found that inclusion was one of the most important predictors of change ownership. And, as we've already noted, coercion, as opposed to participation, tends to lead to "get-even behavior."

If people feel a personal connection to a change and its success, you can pretty much bet they will have a vested interest in seeing it succeed. Additionally, change leaders should remember that while commitment to change begins at the individual level, teams can create lasting change more effectively than individuals. The greater the level of involvement by those affected by a change, the greater their sense of ownership and consequently the greater the likelihood that the change will be embraced and supported.

Now involvement is not possible at all functions of the organization. Very often the setting of the vision of the organization comes from the leadership of that organization. We often say, "the what comes down." But the implementation of that vision must have broad involvement to be successful—"the how comes up." It would be wonderful if the involvement of all employees could be in the "what" and "how," but that often is not possible. Inclusion, however, must involve the "how."

5. People Must Believe They Are Capable of Change

Potency is an essential element for the success of most any change. If people do not believe they are actually capable of making a change, they are more than likely going to resist. Why in the world would I want to risk something new, particularly something I don't believe I have the capacity to do? The probable outcome, at least from this perspective, is that I'm bound to fail. Self-protection is a powerful motivator. If I think I'm going to fail, and as a result look and feel inadequate, incompetent, and worse yet, embarrassed, it's a safe bet I'm going to resist whatever new idea is coming down the pike.

Clance (1986) talks about the imposter phenomenon. It occurs in about 70 percent of competent mangers. It involves feelings of inadequacy— "Everybody else has their stuff together, but I don't. I hope that people don't find out that I am simply pretending. I'm really incompetent." This imposter phenomenon (IP) blocks change, because the possessor of IP believes that their salvation comes in doing the same old things. Change brings the opportunity of being discovered as incompetent. You must believe in yourself if change is to occur.

6. If You Want Lasting Change, Do It Gradually

A critical mistake, one made by many a change agent, is a failure to remember that change is a process; it is not an event. Change, if it is to be successful, should come in stages and not all at once. When you try to push through too much of a major change all at once, you are certain to ensure some major push back in the form of resistance.

As change leaders, we must never overlook the importance of the "theory of small wins." In other words, if we want to increase the long-term success of change, we must ensure that those people impacted by the change experience numerous, smaller, successful changes along the way. You've heard it said before: "success breeds success." The same is true when trying to implement large, major changes.

When large-scale changes are approached incrementally, you can create greater opportunities to build success, and transactional changes can be very instrumental in supporting more transformational change over time. In addition, Harvey (2001) suggests that celebration of change in its early stages can create fertile ground for later stages of change. Approaching change gradually will certainly afford you more opportunities for celebration, and that's a good thing, as you'll see in our next change principle.

7. Whenever Possible, Link Change with Joy

One of the biggest change traps you can fall into as a leader is associating your change effort with doom and gloom. Taking such an "Eeyore" approach to change is sure to set many people running in the opposite direction.

Just imagine if *your* supervisor came to *you* and said, "Oh no, the sky is falling, things are terrible, if we don't make changes all is lost, the world is ending." How excited and motivated would you be to push a change forward? More than likely you'd end up feeling so depressed you wouldn't be able to find the energy to move at all. It's hard to motivate people from the doldrums.

Now don't get us wrong, creating a sense of urgency can and often is a critical step in a successful change process. However, just as success breeds success, change linked with joy and excitement is more apt to occur than changes that are tied to heavy feelings of crisis, disaster, or pending doom.

Creating an aura of anticipation and excitement, generating and demonstrating a genuine sense of enthusiasm, does far more to encourage organizational members to embrace the possibility of change than linking it to gravity and seriousness. In fact, the latter approach is sure to generate resistance. The lesson here is this—if you want change, *have a party*!

The role of joy in change simply can't be overlooked. People are more likely to want to join and support new opportunities when they see them as exciting, positive, and FUN. Yes, you heard us correctly: we said fun. And why not? As we've already said, learning and change are inextricably intertwined. After all, learning is about changing behavior—whether it be in how we think, in how we act, or in how our new thinking leads to new actions.

Fun, as Bob Sullo (2007) perceptively suggests, is the payoff for learning. So if you want to increase your chances for implementing successful change—by golly, DON'T make it onerous; rather, make it inviting, and—that's right—make it fun.

8. Never Underestimate the Power of Organizational Culture

Culture. What comes to mind when you hear this word? Does it conjure up images of rituals, norms, and patterns of behavior? Of deeply held shared values? Of values generated over time and deeply entrenched in an organization's fabric? If it does, then you can certainly begin to understand what a powerful influence culture can have when leaders, or for that matter anyone, attempt to implement changes that might be viewed as countercultural by organizational members.

An organization's vision and values portray not only what it stands for but also a profound sense of what its members view as important. Consequently, any proposed change must be seen as congruent with an organization's mission, vision, and values if it has any chance of being successful. After all, if your change flies in the face of our values, you are challenging who we are, or at least who we see ourselves as being.

Changes that seek to modify an existing culture can be very difficult to accomplish. Let's look at an example. Suppose a traditionally hierarchical organization, such as a conservative religious institution, decided to experiment with the idea of a shared leadership approach to decision making. Really, it could happen! In fact, it is happening in the Catholic Church today (Broyles, 2007). Now, it's important to keep in mind that determinations about how decisions are made within organizations are grounded in its culture, and in hierarchical organizations, decision-making authority tends to be held close to the top.

As you might imagine, under these circumstances, any move toward shared leadership would require at least some modification of the organization's culture, and introducing such a model of leadership into an ingrained hierarchical structure could certainly be perceived as very countercultural. As a result, it could easily create a significant perception of loss for those at the top of the hierarchy and hence generate a high level of resistance.

There are two basic lessons to keep in mind with regard to culture and change. The first is this—changing organizational culture requires time. Culture evolves over time, and you can't expect to change it overnight. Not if you want real change.

The second lesson follows the first—gradualism is particularly important when attempting to make cultural changes. In addition to going slowly, be sure to take small steps, and always, always check to ensure that you are not threatening what has been held near and dear, even sacrosanct, to organizational members, lest you find your change effort without any hope of being embraced anytime soon!

9. Top Leadership Support Is a Key Ingredient in Adopting Change

Perhaps this change principle goes without saying, but nevertheless, we feel the need to make it evident. The truth of the matter is this: if the leadership at the top hasn't bought into your change idea, you'll be fighting an uphill battle. The reasons for this are fairly obvious, but worth mentioning all the same.

First, top brass typically control the way in which resources are allocated. If there are no resources provided to enact your change, your change will not be supported. Second, those in positions of power are generally also in positions to either keep or discard innovative ideas and proposed changes long before they ever get off the ground.

And finally, at least for this part of our discussion, leaders come and leaders go. Change supported by one leader may not be supported by the next. The savvy change agent learns early not only to build and maintain support for change from those at the top but also to prime the pump early when the winds of leadership change begin to blow.

So far, we've been talking about how those at the top must support particular changes, if they are to be successful. However, beyond that reality is another—an organization's overall attitude toward change is also deeply influenced by those at the top. As Collins (2001) points out, leaders set the tenor for change. We believe that our newly elected president, Barack Obama, is a good example of this type of change leadership.

President Obama demonstrated early on his understanding that as the proverbial bearer of a vision of change, he must set the attitude toward change. However, he also knows he must allow others latitude in how to bring about these changes if they are to be truly successful.

Consider his approach to working with his cabinet members. While Obama has clearly set both the tone and overall direction for many of the changes he would like to see occur, he has wisely provided room for his cabinet members to refine the definition of those changes. In addition, he has afforded these individuals a strong role in determining just how to bring these changes about. That attitude—of support toward change while empowering individuals to craft the implementation—is another important ingredient for success.

This brings us to another caveat with regard to change leadership emanating from the top, and that is the notion of "grassroots" change. It is truly a romantic idea, one that is held dear by many. However, we would posit that actual grassroots changes never really occur. Why? Because ultimately, change still requires support and leadership from the top, whatever that top may be, to be sustained.

Conceivably, the only real "bottom-up" changes that occur are those resulting from revolution. Yet even then, a revolution is in reality only exchanging one power structure for another. The American Revolution does perhaps provide a limited example of revolution leading to transformational change. Most revolutions, however, do not.

In the world of organizations, effective change leadership relies on a process that leads to transformation, *not* revolution. And transformation occurs as a process of incremental steps, not as the result of a "big bang" and much hoopla. Collins (2001) describes this well in his discussion of his flywheel model. He reminds us of the power of continued, incremental improvement. As people begin to see and experience tangible results, momentum for change grows. The smart change leader knows this. The less enlightened do not. The truth is that, in the end, it is not only essential to have top leadership support for change to be successful, but savvy leadership as well.

10. Building Trusting Relationships Is Key

Building and sustaining an environment of trust is necessary when looking to initiate and sustain change. Imagine how reluctant you would be to embrace changes proposed by someone you don't particularly trust, or whom you fear does not have your best interests in mind. Throughout history such scenarios have played out between unions and managers. Each is hesitant to trust that the other has no hidden agendas, that proposed changes or operational adjustments are really being put forward in good faith, for the good of all.

Beyond trusting that change agents are not proposing things that will cause harm, people need to trust the changes being proposed. After all, if it's such a good idea, why haven't we tried it before? Furthermore, what sort of track record do you, the change leader have, for actually getting things done? How often have you done "right by us" in the past? People want to know these things before they jump on to your particular change bandwagon, before they decide to support your proposals. Consequently, digging the well long before you are thirsty—creating trusting relationships—will serve you well in future change efforts.

And there you have it—our top ten change principles. Of course, as you've already noticed, these principles are all directly connected to what we believe is an overarching principle: *Resistance to change is a natural, inevitable, and POSITIVE aspect of the change process.* After all, as far as we are concerned, without resistance, you really have no change at all!

RESISTANCE TO CHANGE AND CHANGE LITERATURE

Here we are, nearly at the end of our condensed journey through the theory of change. To finish this part of our adventure, let us come full circle, as it were, and glance back at where resistance fits into change theory. We will do this by closing our chapter with five key ideas to remember about resistance, particularly how it can be viewed within the context of embracing a resistance-based approach to the change process.

A Negative Bias Toward Resistance

Historically, there has been, and there continues to be, a strong inclination to view resistance as a negative force or action. Ask anyone about resistance in general, or better yet, why they are resistant to something, and watch how quickly they bristle.

A great example of this phenomenon occurred quite recently, during a research project in which I was exploring the specific reasons various individuals had resisted a particular change. I was startled by the number of sharp responses—not just from survey participants but also from those who reviewed the research instruments. More than just a few evaluators wanted to know why this was such a negative research project. Participants were equally wary. Comments such as "Why are you asking such negative questions?" abounded. In fact, during one administration of the survey, a participant actually yelled at me, charging that this was by far the most negative study she'd ever participated in.

The reality is clear: many, many people still see resistance as a negative force, something that they not only do not want to talk about but also do not want to admit feeling. However, while this negative bias is clearly evident, we ardently believe that resistance is by no means a negative, but rather a positive element of change. Fortunately, this belief is slowly being reflected in a growing body of change literature. We hope that you too will begin to recognize and embrace resistance as a positive, powerful force.

Resistance is Both a Natural and an Essential Element of Change

As we've hopefully made evident, resistance is a natural element of the change process and every change effort creates some level of resistance. Many have even argued that our very biological makeup holds an inherent, built-in resistance response, that we are in fact programmed not to change (Black and Gregerson, 2002).

However, beyond being a natural element of change, we suggest it is really an essential component. Without resistance, you cannot have real growth. Tension leads to change as we adapt to new circumstances and settings. In reality, change without resistance is no change at all, but merely an illusion of change (Harvey, 2001).

Resistance Occurs at All Stages of the Change Process

While it is certainly true that addressing resistance during the first phase of a change process (the unfreezing stage) is critical (how else would you move anywhere, after all?), it would be a mistake to assume this is the only place resistance must be considered. Resistance can and does occur at all phases of the change process, from unfreezing to moving, and even as you attempt to refreeze. In fact, Lippitt, Watson, and Westly (1958) noted that even the mere act of diagnosing an organization's readiness for and resistance to change can itself generate resistance.

This reality, that resistance can be present throughout the process, is why it is critical for change leaders to not only diagnose and plan for those resistance factors likely to be in play early in a change effort but also consider potential sources throughout the process. That means engaging in ongoing evaluation and adjustments. Remember, change is a process, NOT an event.

At this juncture it bears mentioning that there are some change experts who have vociferously called into question the value of planned change. They suggest that the frequent failure of change efforts is proof positive that new models are required. We would beg to slightly differ. We do not believe planned change is the culprit. Rather, we believe that change fails primarily because we do not adequately or effectively plan for resistance! What we really need are resistance-based models of change. And that, of course, is the premise that undergirds our approach to implementing change.

A Resistance-Based Approach to Change

For any change effort to succeed, resistance must be addressed. Remember what we said a few moments ago—you can't unfreeze if resistance keeps you stuck in your tracks. Addressing resistance requires three very important steps. First, you must diagnose or analyze what sources of resistance may occur at various stages of a change process. This is a step many a change leader fails to do, and the consequences are often terminal.

Next, you must plan for that resistance. You must strategize. Strategies are systematic plans for creating change, plans that are specifically aligned with the particular change environment. Beyond selecting the right strategies, it is vital to apply them at the right time. In fact, these two nuggets are two of the most important pieces of any resistance-based approach to change: select the right strategies and apply the right strategies at the right time.

Apply the Right Strategies at the Right Time

This final piece, applying strategies at the right time, also makes the case for the importance of engaging in an ongoing evaluation of the change process. Such an approach allows you to make adjustments, in both timing and strategies, as the circumstances warrant.

There are a number of benefits to embarking on a resistance-based approach to change, not the least of which is that such an approach will increase the likelihood of success. However, with all this said, you certainly can't embark on a resistance-based approach to change without developing an understanding of what potential sources of resistance you are likely to encounter.

SOURCES OF RESISTANCE

There are many ways to look at sources of resistance to change. Some authors present a few broad categories, others focus on individual versus organizational sources, and still others address behaviors and sources at the same time. We prefer to discuss resistance in terms of specific, discrete sources. While we are not suggesting this is the only way, we have found this categorization method to be the most effective for our purposes.

We propose twenty discrete sources of resistance that change agents might consider as they diagnose their organization's readiness for change/sources of resistance.

These sources include:

- Lack of Ownership
- Lack of Benefits
- Increased Burdens
- Lack of Top Brass Support
- Loneliness
- Insecurity

- Norm Incongruence
- Boredom
- Chaos
- Superiority
- Differential Knowledge
- Lack of Recognition
- Sudden Wholesale Change
- Fear of Failure
- Extremes of Organizational Structure
- Lack of Trust/Suspicion
- Ambiguity
- Lack of Leadership Skills
- Inertia
- Referent Power

In the following chapters we will describe each of the above sources of resistance, suggest antidotes, and provide you with strategies for assessing the potential presence of each resistance factor within your own organizations.

Part II

RESISTANCE FACTORS

CHAPTER 3

Resistance Factor 1: Lack of Ownership

Steven had no investment in the change. He had merely been on the side-lines while the managers of the plan had devised the new warehouse system. He didn't care whether it succeeded or not. It made no difference to him. Well, to think on it, he hoped that it would fail. After all, he was comfortable with the way things were now. Who were the "suits" to tell him how to warehouse supplies? The old ways worked most of the time and the old ways were inefficient enough to keep him busy. He would wait until the new system would fail. He might even sabotage it. He had been there for twenty-two years, and they weren't going to tell him what to do.

Steven had no investment in the change because he had not participated in its creation. People resist a change that they have not had any chance to create. There is an old adage that says, "The *what* comes down and the *how* comes up." By this we mean that in most organizations, the vision of change, the *what*, is provided by leadership of the organization. It is their responsibility to define the vision. But it must be the responsibility of the line workers or teachers or the staff to define *how* it's going to be brought about. If the staff merely inherit the change without any participation in the *how* or *what* of the change, they will resist it like Steven did. It would be nice if the staff could be involved in defining both the *what* and *how* of change, but that isn't always practical. But they must be involved in creating the *how*.

It's just like home ownership. If you own it (you've bought it), you mow the grass and do the house repairs. You'll reroof it if it needs it and you may even add on to it. But if you're renting it, you're not as likely to take care of it. You'll let the grass grow longer and you'll not repair the roof. You'll let someone else do it. Ownership has tremendous benefits most people.

In an organization ownership comes from participation. When you're on a committee to define the change in a warehouse system, you have a say in how you're going to implement it, you gain ownership in the change. It may not be that any of the solutions are novel or unique. It may not be the quality of your decision is any better than the manager's. But merely by participating you will gain involvement and, hence, ownership.

I remember when I was called in to be a consultant on a change project by a large milk company. They had undue breakage of milk bottles on the line (I'm dating myself, aren't I?). So they got a bunch of engineers together to design a new crating system. The engineers were successful, so they put it into effect on the line. Well, rather than going down, breakage went up. The engineers were baffled. This is where I came in.

I went down on the line and took some of the men out for ice cream sundaes. They eventually came clean (with the help of a sugar high) and confessed that they were breaking the bottles. As they said, "Why do the 'suits' have any business in telling us how to run the line?" They did not have ownership, so they resisted the change. So I went back up to the "suits" and asked them to give me authority to get the staff together and devise a better crating system. To make a long story short, they gave me the time, the men designed a new crating system, and breakage went way down. The crates weren't any better than those of the engineers, but they were theirs.

What's the moral of our story? Participation leads to ownership. Ownership overcomes resistance. You *may* be involved in designing the *what* of change. You *must* be involved in the *how*. If you are not involved in the *what* or the *how*, if you are only left to stand on the sidelines, two things are very likely to happen. First, you are free to avoid any responsibility for the outcome. After all, it wasn't your idea, you didn't have a hand in it, so how could you possibly be accountable for how it works out? Second, and just as likely, as evidenced by our story, you may even feel inclined to engage in a little (or a lot) of sabotage of the change.

Consequently, even if, in all good intention, as the change leader you tell people both the *what* and the *how* of change, you shoot yourself in the foot, not once but twice. You not only rob the staff of an opportunity to design the change, and potentially grow in the process, but also increase the chances for sabotage and failure.

The reality is, like it or not, if you want change to occur, you must delegate the *how* of change. We aren't talking about wholesale delegation. That can be just as costly and ineffective as having no participation at all. Rather, you must carefully plan and craft the way in which you delegate responsibility for designing a particular change. In doing so, leaders must also remain cognizant of just how much people can digest or accomplish at any one time. After all, while part of your goal is clearly to develop a sense of ownership, you must also consider how to build in a level of positive accomplishment. Remember, success breeds success.

Finally, when it comes to delegation, and consequently creating a true sense of ownership, it is essential to remember that people are imperfect. Forget this fact and you will likely find yourself sorely disappointed. However, keep this in mind and you may be pleasantly surprised. In the end, the goal of a good manager is to work toward continuous improvement, while accepting imperfection. After all, if you are only willing to promote ownership that is built upon an unobtainable level of perfection, all of the participation in the world won't move your change any further forward, and in the end it may actually do more harm than good.

Resistance Factor 1	*Antidote*
Lack of Ownership	Participation in What or How

QUESTIONS TO BE ASKED BY THE CHANGE AGENT

Did you participate in crafting the change? If yes, how?

CHAPTER 4

Resistance Factor 2:
Lack of Top Brass Support

Fred really liked his colleague's idea. Using their electronic calendars to set up appointments and sharing them so that they could easily see when people were available and in or out of the office would really improve their efficiency. He himself had often wished they used technology more to their advantage. BUT he also knew that their department director was NOT into technology at all. In fact, Fred was fairly sure that the director would put the kibosh on this idea in a hurry. While Fred wanted to support his colleague, he just knew that the idea wasn't going to go anywhere. Instead of rocking the boat, he continued to set up his appointments "the old-fashioned way," calling his colleagues and wasting time waiting for return calls.

"I don't think the boss will like this." That simplest of statements is a sure sign that resistance is in the air. It's the very type of resistance Fred's colleague was about to encounter, the kind of resistance that bubbles up due to lack of support for change from those higher up in the organization.

The reality is that most people in an organization will not willingly go along with proposed changes unless they feel assured that those individuals vested with the responsibility for overseeing organizational goals also support the change (Harvey, 2001). This realization flies in the face of our often dearly held notion that much change begins at the grassroots level.

In actuality, while this may occasionally be true, in most circumstances you are unlikely to get real movement toward change without the support of those higher up the food chain. Additionally, this support must be clear AND overt. Behind-the-scenes words of encouragement will hardly be the leverage needed to move resistors and skeptics forward.

Why is top brass support so important? Well, for starters, consider that those at the top often control organizational resources—the very resources you may need to start or sustain your change. In the case of Fred's colleague, one of the resources—their electronic calendars—already existed. However, Fred's director also controlled an often overlooked resource—time. Time was required if Fred's department was going to learn how to use their electronic calendars in this new way. If the director was not willing to allocate that time, the likelihood of the change actually taking off was virtually nil. The truth is, if the will to change does not exist further up the ladder, the change is often dead on arrival. The hard reality is that organizational elites can resist or discard changes long before they ever have any hope of taking off.

So how do we garner top brass support? The answer—we borrow from what we already know about change theory. Ask yourself, what is the perceived payoff for the upper echelon? Remember—we already know what we think the payoff will be for us, BUT we must identify the payoff for the resistor.

In Fred's case the payoff for the resistant director might be greater unit productivity, which could in turn lead to bonuses for department leaders (a.k.a. the director) down the line. However, that may prove to be just a bit too altruistic to be viable, or the payoff might be too far off in the distance to be immediately attractive. What if, on the other hand, Fred's colleague could find a way to make the director think the change was really his idea—that the director came up with it on his own? Under those circumstances, the idea has a much better chance of gaining traction.

I once found myself in just such a situation, while working for a non-profit organization many years ago. Our communication with our field offices was dismal. I knew that networking our satellite offices with our main office would pay huge dividends in improved internal communication. However, I also knew that our director would resist such a suggestion. She was notorious for her propensity to champion only those ideas for which she could take direct credit. I had to work strategically, planting seeds whenever the opportunity arose, but never suggesting the change outright. In the end, she ultimately "discovered" the idea, promoted it to the board of directors, and led the charge for implementation.

The outcome was truly a win-win for all of us. Not only was the director credited with the idea, she actually felt ownership for it as well. And those of us on the front lines? Having access to faster, more reliable communication technology definitely made our jobs easier!

Another way to generate top-level support might involve looking for or even creating a sense of urgency. Perhaps the organization finds itself needing to move quickly on an upcoming opportunity. Meetings need to be scheduled, decisions need to be made—and quickly. BUT, alas, precious time is being wasted trying to figure out who is available and when. Now would be the opportune time to make your suggestion. "Hey, boss. You know, if we were to try sharing our electronic calendars, why, we'd be able to instantly see who is available and when and really streamline the process." Voilà, your change becomes a possible solution to an urgent situation. Once the value of the change is seen and success is demonstrated, your boss's openness to trying it again increases.

Another approach to dealing with resistant top brass involves the co-option of someone close to the boss, a trusted advisor to the boss. Nurturing a change advocate, one whose advice is trusted by those higher up, can create just the right environment for the boss to at least be open to the idea. Trust is a powerful force, as we discuss in our chapter on referent power, and if you can enlist the support of someone the boss trusts, you may be one step closer to moving your change idea forward.

We need to add a word of caution at this point, because it is essential to recognize that top brass support is insufficient, on its own, to sustain a change. Leaders come and leaders go—and leaders change their minds. For example, Senge (1999) points out, change initiated or pushed forward under an authoritarian banner will decelerate once the interest of the authoritarian diminishes, or after he or she has moved on to greener pastures.

If you want your change to last, and to protect it from the changing winds of leadership turnover, you must work to institutionalize it—and not after the fact, but rather during your planning and implementation stages. We discuss this in more detail in chapter 24, but suffice it to say here that one must plan with the end in mind—that is, with institutionalization as a long-range goal.

Resistance Factor 2	*Antidote*
Lack of Top Brass Support	• Top Brass Support
	• Payoff for Top Brass
	• Co-option of Trusted Advocates to the Brass

QUESTIONS TO BE ASKED BY THE CHANGE AGENT

To what degree do you think that the organizational leadership supports this change? Why or why not?

CHAPTER 5

Resistance Factor 3: Lack of Benefits

Clare could not think of a single reason why she should adhere to the new lunchtime policy being implemented at the childcare center where she worked as a lead teacher. What exactly did the director think would be gained by expecting Clare and the other teachers to actually start sitting with the children during mealtime? For as long as Clare could remember, she and the other childcare staff always stood together and chatted while the children sat at their little tables and ate their lunch. As far as Clare was concerned, this system worked just fine, thank you very much! It's not as though the children weren't monitored. Besides, this arrangement gave her a few minutes of reprieve. Not only did she get a break from constantly interacting with the children, it gave her a little time to visit with her co-workers. Just exactly what was in it for her if she was now going to have to sit with the children? She might do it when she knew the director was around, but she'd be darned if she was going to do it when the director wasn't around!

All change is loss, at least for someone. Clare not only saw a loss in what she had come to view as her built-in free time but also saw no clear benefit *for her* in going along with this new policy. As a result, she was resistant.

One of the most common sources of resistance occurs when there is a lack of perceived payoff *for the changee*. People resist change when they do not see any obvious advantages *for them*. This is only sane, but it is something many change leaders misunderstand. Far too often change agents assume that just because the payoff for a change seems wonderful to them (it will be great for the bottom line, it will be good for the children), somehow those affected by the change will automatically perceive things in the same way. NO! Any benefits for a change must be perceived as valuable to the changee, NOT just the change agent.

Although Clare's center director was certain the new policy would have great benefit for the children, she inadvertently assumed that her staff would automatically be swayed by such a logical argument. Unfortunately, the director overlooked two very important things: (1) Clare's sense of loss, and (2) her perception that there was no benefit to her personally. Had the director asked Clare what she thought about the new policy, listened to her concerns, and come up with a way that Clare could identify meaningful benefits, things may have happened differently.

Several years ago, I worked with an early childhood center that experienced a similar situation. The new director genuinely believed that having teachers sit with the children during meals would have many benefits; it would create more of a family atmosphere, increase social interactions, and positively influence the children's language development. These were certainly all worthy goals. I mean, who could argue with them?

The director was completely caught off guard by the level of resistance she encountered from the teachers. She simply could not understand why they would be so unmotivated by such obviously valuable payoffs for the children. Her mistake was twofold—she not only failed to anticipate the sense of loss her teachers might feel but also did not identify or articulate any meaningful advantages *for the teachers* themselves.

After just a few days of observing, it was fairly obvious that whenever the director was in the vicinity during mealtimes the teachers would, albeit grudgingly, sit with the children. However, as soon as the director wasn't around, the teachers reverted to their old habits.

A few weeks into our regularly scheduled staff development sessions, I took advantage of an evening the director wasn't present and broached the subject of the new policy. It didn't take long before the teachers aired their grievances over the new policy. Much like Clare, they felt like there wasn't really any added value for them.

Now don't get me wrong, it wasn't that the teachers didn't care about the children; they most certainly did. However, the loss they felt was very real to them, and, at least as far as they could see, nothing had been added to offset that loss. Do you remember what we said in chapter 2, about going from point A to point B? Point B has to be something that the changee sees as attractive—someplace they WANT to go toward. In this scenario, that had been, up until now, overlooked.

I decided to embark on a brainstorming activity with the teachers. It took some coaxing, but eventually someone offered up the idea that if teachers were to sit with the children, they would be right there to help the little ones when they needed more milk or a second serving. Another brave soul suggested there might be fewer incidences of children wandering away from the table and the tantrum that often ensued once a teacher noticed and insisted that the child return to the table.

After a while the teachers began to identify several possible ways the new policy might actually have a payoff for them, particularly in time gained. For example, fewer tantrums might translate into a smoother transition to naptime. That could mean a longer period of "quiet" time for the teachers to visit and complete paperwork. Now that sounded like a payoff the teachers could get their hands around! They agreed to give the new policy a fair shake.

Now don't be fooled into thinking that everything ran as smooth as a well-oiled machine right away. Many changes go through what Fullan (2007) refers to as the "implementation dip." It takes a while for the payoff to be clear and relatively consistent, and sometimes we are tempted to slide back into old habits if we don't see results right away. However, the important point here is that when the right incentives are identified and implemented with an eye toward recognizing and building on successes, the resistance that occurs because of a perceived lack of benefits FOR THE CHANGEE can indeed be overcome!

Resistance Factor 3	*Antidote*
Lack of Benefits	Meaningful Payoff

QUESTIONS TO BE ASKED BY THE CHANGE AGENT

In what ways do you see the new change as beneficial to you and the work you currently do?

In what ways might it add value?

What would you need to have so that the change provided you with more of a benefit?

CHAPTER 6

Resistance Factor 4: Lack of Recognition

All Allan wanted was a little recognition. He wasn't asking for much. He saw the need for change and even approached his boss about the problem. Now a solution was being proposed without his input or participation. His boss didn't even recognize him for identifying the problem. Heck, the change wasn't even a very good solution to the problem. He would subtly oppose it and maybe even sabotage it a little. He was already late to the meeting that they were going to use to announce it. He didn't care. Oh well, at least he didn't have to take any responsibility for the solution. That's the plus side of not getting any recognition. He didn't have to assume any responsibility for the problem's solution. He entered the meeting and took a seat away from the table. He crossed his arms and just listened, but really didn't hear.

Allan was experiencing the effects of both sides of nonrecognition. First of all, he was suffering from a lack of positive recognition. Herzberg, Mausner, and Snyderman (1959) tell us that one of the prime elements of job satisfaction is recognition. Allan wasn't given any public congratulations for identifying the problem nor was he given any role in coming up with the solution. Allan's boss worked on the supposition that Allan was self-motivated and didn't need any recognition. He, like so many of us, was dead wrong. Without celebration of people and their ideas, there is resistance to change. Why should they go "out on a limb" to make your change work when you can't even manage to motivate them correctly? In an environment where recognition does not flourish, there is no change.

Secondly, Allan was experiencing the relief of no responsibility for the change. When there is no recognition of your contribution in the change effort—either in identifying the problem or negotiating its resolution—you can hide. You can avoid any responsibility for it. For many that is a welcome relief. But for the organization that is a terrible waste of human capital. A lack of responsibility allows people to stay "fat, dumb, and happy." That's a comfortable place to be, but not very satisfying or productive.

This lack of recognition manifests itself in many negative ways. It shows up in being chronically late for meetings, side-talking, chain rattling, indifference to new ideas, asking a million pointless questions, never volunteering for anything, sniping and passive-aggressive behavior, and general sabotage of all positive behavior. These negative actions are cues for positive recognition of peoples' contributions to the corporate effort. However, when these cues are missed or overlooked, it can be detrimental for more than just a few people. I am reminded of a situation that illustrates this reality well.

There once was a young faculty member on our academic senate. He was bright and enthusiastic and offered up many new ideas. Regrettably, no one ever supported or even recognized his ideas. As time went by and he was consistently ignored, his behavior began to shift. Instead of generating ideas, he became an obstructionist, disagreeing with, opposing, and even sabotaging everyone else's ideas. In fact, he became fairly well known as a royal pain in the behind, at least by many of the senior faculty. In many ways, by their own actions, or in this case inaction, the faculty had bred their own worst enemy.

After his first term ended, our young faculty member decided to run for a second. Now you might expect that, given his reputation, his second bid would be unsuccessful. Wrong! He was indeed elected a second time, but by a very unique constituency—the "anti-anything" faculty. Every organization has such a group, and this young man had endeared himself to them through his persistent obstinate, negative behavior. Unfortunately, the end result was a lose-lose situation for almost everyone involved. You see, eventually, this once ambitious, forward-thinking faculty member came up for tenure. Alas, he had so alienated himself from the senior faculty—the very political allies he needed—that they denied him this advancement, not because of lack of merit, but rather because he had become so unlikeable. In the end, he'd sabotaged himself as well.

So what's a leader to do? How do we overcome, or better yet, avoid this lack of recognition? Consider what might have happened if only the president of the senate had taken our young man under his wing and given him some kudos, some recognition, for his efforts and his ideas.

As leaders, it is absolutely critical that you actively think about how to give positive recognition, so that people can become productive instead of oppositional and counterproductive. For starters, we suggest you keep a scorecard of whom you recognize and how. Every month you go over your scorecard to look to see if you've done enough celebration, public congratulations, and thanks. That makes for good management and, thus, for good change.

Secondly, you need to include people in the change process. But not just the same old faces. Include your resistors and hiders. In the act of participation they will no longer act as resistors or hiders. Through recognition you accomplish much. It is said that there can't be too much recognition. Praise motivates toward top performance.

The trouble is that managers tend to get too busy and don't keep a scorecard on celebration and praise. They figure that people management should take a backseat to task management. To do so is to manage badly. The leadership of change requires you to recognize and celebrate. In this way bad behavior is shaped into good behavior, and after a while you don't get so much resistance to change.

Resistance Factor 4	*Antidote*
Lack of Recognition	• Recognition Scorecard
	• Celebration
	• Participation

QUESTIONS TO BE ASKED BY THE CHANGE AGENT

Do you get recognized for your contribution to this organization?

Does your organization celebrate your ideas and actions?

Do you have any participation in identifying or solving the problems in your organization? How much?

CHAPTER 7

Resistance Factor 5: Increased Burdens

Inez hated that she had to shift from her familiar WordPerfect software to the unfamiliar and, as far as she was concerned, more complex Works program. It would take a lot more time to learn how to use the new software, and she just didn't have that kind of time. Maybe in the future, but certainly not now. She was doing everything else but taking the time to learn the new program. She knew it, but she was too old to learn new tricks. Maybe she could outwait the "suits." She was a valuable employee, and surely they wouldn't make her do it.

Anything that increases one's burdens will be resisted. Whether it increases the time you must give or the money you will expend or the energy you will have to put out or the added skills you will have to learn, you will act with resentment to the change. If you're forced to make the change, you will either sabotage it or find ways to undermine the change effort. If you're not forced to make the change, you will not do it. You will successfully resist it.

Changes that increase a person's workload, or that are perceived as being more burdensome than the previous way of conducting business, are bound for a collision course with the resistance train. Consequently, change leaders are well advised to do two very important things.

First, and perhaps obviously, they must be able to effectively express the upside of implementing a proposed change. However, this is not enough. Why? Because it only identifies the benefits from one perspective, that of the person pushing the change. The second, and even more crucial, task is to help others, particularly those most affected by the change, to identify and articulate their own potential payoffs. The reality is, if others cannot see how the change will benefit them, they aren't likely to embrace a change willingly. Let's look at Inez and her resistance to a new word processing program in order to illustrate this point.

Poor Inez. She was faced with a change she was quite certain would not only place a significant burden on her already overcommitted time, but would also require her to learn new skills. On top of that, she could not even remotely see how the new software would save her any time in the future. You see, Inez was very *present*-oriented. She was focused solely on the here and now. The burden she was concerned with was here, in the present. She could not even begin to adequately consider the future. At the moment, the only future she could envision was one in which she outwitted the "suits."

The solution to Inez's problem is twofold. First, Inez must be *enticed* to make the change. How can this be done? You must identify a motivational reward—but not just any reward. The reward must be one that is motivational TO INEZ. Such a reward can only be successfully discovered by having a discussion directly *with* Inez. You must ask her what would be motivational and rewarding to her!

There are a variety of options. Perhaps she would appreciate additional compensation. It could be that some time off would be seen as an adequate reward for the time required to learn the ins and outs of this new software package. Maybe she would consider the offer of a gym membership as a valued reward. Whatever it is, it must be a reward, a payoff *for her*. People are not likely to change, at least not willingly for any sustained period of time, unless they can identify a clear payoff, one that is *meaningful for them*.

As you strive to uncover the right motivational reward, or perhaps combination of rewards, it bears keeping the work of Herzberg, Mausner, and Snyderman (1959) in mind. In their well-known research into motivation, work, and job satisfaction, Herzberg and his colleagues identified a series of factors which can serve as motivators in the workforce. These factors are divided into two categories:

- "satisfiers"—those factors that can enrich a job, and that when present can induce more and sustained effort, potentially even leading to improved performance, and
- "dissatisfiers"—those factors that, when absent, can create dissatisfaction with a job, and may even result in someone leaving the organization.

Satisfiers	Dissatisfiers
• Recognition	• Interpersonal Relations
• Achievement	• Facilities
• Responsibility	• Money (salary, benefits, etc.)
	• Security

Figure 7.1. *List of Satisfiers/Dissatisfiers*

For the purposes of this discussion, and in order to focus our conversation more specifically on motivational rewards in the context of meaningful payoffs in a change environment, we have condensed Herzberg's original list of satisfiers and dissatisfiers. These are included in figure 7.1.

So how do these factors apply for the change leader searching for an intervention, a strategy to address resistance to a change perceived to increase the burdens of an employee? Each of the factors listed in figure 7.1 reflects a potential area for payoff. For example, perhaps as Inez becomes an expert in the new software program, she may be given new responsibilities—such as training others or serving as the "go to" person. Now, if Inez values such levels of responsibility, this could be the motivation she needs to embrace the change. Perhaps Inez values recognition for her efforts to learn the new program. This recognition could come in the form of an award, public acknowledgment for taking a leadership role in learning the new system, or even lunch with the boss. Of course the underlying element is that the payoff for getting on board must be perceived as valuable to Inez. And how will you know? You have to ask her!

Before we move on in our discussion, there are a few salient points to consider when working with Herzberg and colleagues' list of satisfiers and dissatisfiers. First, satisfiers are directly related to what a person *does*—the *content* of the work. Dissatisfiers concern the *context* of the work, the *environment* in which the job is done. This is relevant in that as a leader, you must be cognizant of those things over which you actually have influence to change, to offer in terms of a meaningful payoff.

Second, according to Herzberg and colleagues' findings, it is the satisfiers that lead to more long-term positive effects in job performance, whereas addressing dissatisfiers has a tendency to result only in short-term changes in performance, which can quickly revert back to earlier behaviors and outputs. For example, what if the dissatisfier is a sense that one's job is not secure because of a proposed change? Finding a way to assuage this sense of insecurity may lead to a temporary willingness to embrace a change, but for how long?

Finally, and perhaps most surprisingly, monetary rewards, such as increases in salary, fringe benefits, and the like, actually have more potency as a dissatisfier than a satisfier. Why? Because oftentimes people tend to feel they should have been compensated at this "new" rate to begin with, hence the motivational power to continue with the increased performance or changed behavior can wane rather quickly. Nevertheless, as with the other factors in Herzberg and colleagues' model, each can serve as a potential source of motivation and potential payoff for the employee feeling reluctant to embrace a change due to a sense of increased burdens.

The chart in figure 7.2 can be used as a simple assessment tool as you explore potential areas of satisfiers, dissatisfiers, and possible payoff for various resistors.

Keep in mind as you go through the identification of potentially motivational rewards that any payoff is, in the end, really twofold. First, employees may discover a benefit that outweighs their sense of burden, and second, as a result the change effort may move forward. Finally, it is likely, if not highly probable, that if at least one of these motivational

Motivational Factor	Employee Issue Yes/No	Potential Actions
Satisfier		
• Recognition		
• Achievement		
• Responsibility		
Dissatisfier		
• Interpersonal Relations		
• Facilities		
• Money		
• Security		

Figure 7.2.   *Assessment Tool for Satisfiers/Dissatisfiers*

payoffs is not addressed when an employee balks at a proposed change, the odds are that a sense of increased burden will be an influential source of resistance to change.

Let's return to Inez one last time and examine our earlier suggestion that the solution to her overall problem was twofold. We've already talked about the first solution—finding a motivational reward. Now let's explore the second. To reduce Inez's resistance, she also needs to acquire any new or required skills in small, baby steps. It is important to break down the task into small units, expect Inez to acquire only one or two of the units at a time, and provide the time to accomplish these steps. Remember the theory of small wins. In addition, you must remember to reward or recognize the acquisition of small, baby steps. The accumulation of successive small wins increases potency, further decreases resistance, and ultimately increases your chances for success.

The antidote to increased burdens is this, much as we have described in our discussion of Inez and her situation:

1. Provision of payoffs—whether in terms of money, time, energy, and skills, one or more of these must be attended to
2. Achievement of the change in small steps

If you implement one or both of these strategies, you'll overcome people's resistance to change due to feeling burdened. (These concepts are also addressed in detail in our chapter on fear of failure. Please refer to this chapter for further explanation.)

Resistance Factor 5	*Antidote*
Increased Burdens	• Payoffs
	• Small Steps

QUESTIONS TO BE ASKED BY THE CHANGE AGENT

What does the change cost you in terms of:

a. Time
b. Money
c. Energy
d. Skills?

What payoffs can we give you in terms of:

a. Recognition
b. Achievement
c. Responsibility
d. Interpersonal Relations
e. Facilities
f. Money
g. Security?

CHAPTER 8

Resistance Factor 6: Loneliness

Herb's boss loved to be on the cutting edge, always eager to be the first one "on the block" to try something new. In fact, it seemed like every time she came back from a conference or a meeting she had a new idea that they just had to implement. The last conference was no different. The boss dropped her latest "state-of-the-art" bomb on them during their Monday morning staff meeting. She went on and on about how exciting the new technique was and that it was really great because they were absolutely going to be the first ones to try it! Herb groaned. "Oh great," he thought, "Just what I need!" Exactly where was he going to be able to go if he had trouble? If no one else was using this "great new" technique, how was he supposed to know if they were even doing it right? Herb was beginning to feel more than a little bit apprehensive about the whole idea. As a matter of fact, he could already envision himself dragging his feet.

Loneliness—that gnawing sense of discomfort that creeps in when people are asked to make cutting-edge changes, things so new that few others have implemented them, which call on them to leave behind the safety of their "collegial cocoon." This is exactly what Herb was experiencing, and his poor boss was clueless. She didn't have the slightest inkling of what was coming—that's right, resistance was about to rear its head. You might mistakenly think that folks would inherently be excited about being on the front line of innovation. Surprising as it may be, the reality is that resistance frequently occurs when you begin asking people to do things that are VERY DIFFERENT, not only from what THEY are used to doing, but from what their PEERS are doing as well.

Consider what might go through your own mind if management announced that next month your department was going to adopt a brand-new process, one that no one else had tried before. You might think, "Hey, maybe that's just dandy for the crew of the Starship Enterprise with their whole 'to boldly go where no man has gone before' thing, BUT at least they didn't go ALONE. They had each other. I, on the other hand, am not so wild about being out there on the edge of the world. Exactly where is *my* safety net going to be? Where are *my* fellow crewmates?"

When people sense that a change will take them away from the support or collegiality of their peers, they can quickly begin to feel isolated and alone. Add to that the possibility of few, if any, available models to show them what this new thing looks like. They can easily become overwhelmed, unsure of what to do or where to begin. In response, seeking to maintain their sense of safety and camaraderie, they often begin traveling down the road of resistance.

Perhaps the best and most obvious antidote to loneliness is to provide opportunities for collegiality. How? We suggest that one of the most effective ways to accomplish this is through the formation of change teams—those teams empowered with the task of moving a change forward. In fact, the expanse of literature on learning communities is replete with examples illustrating the benefits of creating such teams to foster innovation and champion change efforts. Teams provide a sense of mutual support, collaboration, and shared learning.

Consider how things may have gone differently for Herb if his boss had formed a team to explore the new technique she was most recently enamored with. Instead of dropping a bomb at the Monday meeting, what if she had announced her plan to bring together a team to learn more about the technique she had heard about? What if this team were tasked with learning all they could about the technique, discussing its benefits and barriers, and examining its possible fit with the organization? Perhaps they might even be asked to experiment with a pilot program, a test run, a trial balloon. The response to the idea of change may have been far different.

The creation of a change team could engender several benefits for Herb's boss and for the organization. For example, teams can create a sense of collegiality and collaboration (valuable antidotes to loneliness), as well as a sense of ownership and even advocacy for the change. The change is no longer the boss's alone, but the team's as well.

Additionally, if the team were empowered to float a trial balloon, to pilot the technique, they could introduce a modicum of gradualism, further alleviating loneliness by creating an evolving feeling of success and consequently potency.

These benefits would have the combined effect of reducing the resistance that so often occurs when people feel too far out on the cutting edge. Herb would be more inclined to at least consider the change, and his boss would have a far greater chance of having the new technique implemented. Finally, such a team might even protect the boss from adopting a technique that actually proved to be a poor fit for the organization after all!

Resistance Factor 6	*Antidote*
Loneliness	• Collegiality
	• Change Teams
	• Gradualism

QUESTIONS TO BE ASKED BY THE CHANGE AGENT

What is your current level of comfort and confidence with adopting this new change? Why?

Do you have an adequate role model to follow to implement the change?

Are you aware of others who have adopted this change? How do you feel about their situation?

CHAPTER 9

Resistance Factor 7: Insecurity

Jane looked at the proposed new accounting software system. It was very good. It was so good, in fact, that they wouldn't need her any longer in about a year or so. She felt threatened. She had worked for the company for twelve years, and she didn't want to seek employment again. This new system had to be stopped. She saw that it had a few glitches in it and she could capitalize on them to bring dissatisfaction with the new accounting system. In that way, they would go back to the old system, where she was needed. Her boss told her that her job might be changing, but she would still be needed. She didn't believe him. He was looking to get rid of her. But she wasn't going so easily.

If security is threatened, then there is no change or at least the sabotage of the change effort begins. Maslow (1970) has long written about the need for security. Without it nothing else will happen. Security is, in fact, at the base of his self-actualization theory. Herzberg, Mausner, and Snyderman (1959) have often written about the need for the hygiene factors to be met before any other factors can be addressed. Chief among these is security, both physical and psychic. If you're in a physically unsafe school where violence is always around the corner, then nothing else matters until you solve the safety issues. If you're in a psychic security issue, such as the one Jane is in, then nothing else matters. Job security comes first.

Let me hasten to add at this point that insecurity may be real or just perceived. It doesn't matter. Cognitive dissonance theory holds that we are just as likely to act whether it is real or perceived. You operate in the same way. You may hide. You may sabotage the system. You may even quit. But surely you will not be interested in some change, other than that which improves your security.

Conversely, what if you're secure in your job? Then a change comes along that threatens your security, whether real or perceived. You will resist it, just as Jane did. Change that threatens security, or change done in an environment where insecurity already exists, will be resisted.

It should be noted that there are also times when insecurity has been wielded as the preferred tool of the Machiavellian leader. Such leaders have been known to intentionally employ strategies with the sole aim of generating a sense of insecurity. Why? In order to cement the current status quo. We need not look far into history to find evidence of such tactics emanating from Hugo Chávez, the president of Venezuela. He is firmly anti-American, because such policies lead to a unified populace. The enemy without keeps the people from looking at the enemy within.

Our past presidents were not immune to the strategy. Consider the use of fear as a policy. Heightening the level of fear was a strategy frequently drawn upon by George W. Bush. Repeatedly generating a sense of threat, of perceived fear, fueled a constant sense of insecurity. Why would this be considered beneficial? Because it brings people together, circling the wagons around the status quo. We can't change our strategies, or even explore options—that's too dangerous. We must instead stay our current course. Fear and insecurity can be used to cement people in place and generate great resistance toward change.

Of course, it isn't just the so-called Machiavellian types that may use insecurity as a vehicle to stay the status quo. Consider one of our other presidents—FDR. Franklin Delano Roosevelt, beloved by many, is also believed to have drawn upon insecurity as a calculated strategy. Many historians have argued that FDR intentionally used certain events of World War II to both consolidate his own power and to bring people together. For example, while Roosevelt spoke publicly about his desire to keep America out of the war, he might have known in advance of the planned attack on Pearl Harbor, yet chose not to act to stop it (Stinnet, 2000). Why? It has been widely asserted that he wanted to incite our involvement in the war. Allowing the attack to move forward served to generate a sense of common enemy, a very powerful vehicle for bringing people together, making them more cohesive.

Creating an intense sense of being under threat and having common enemies often serves to pull people together, to protect their way of doing things, to maintain the status quo. And in so doing, we often abdicate our personal power and entrust someone else to "protect" us. The truth is, by emphasizing insecurity many a leader has been able to cement his or her own power.

Insecurity. It tends to hold us frozen in place. We vehemently fight change and anything that could be perceived as a threat to our well-being. While there are those who use this strategy to promote their own agendas, we do not advocate such behavior. Rather, our interests are in how to address that sense of insecurity that arises when we introduce changes we believe are for the betterment of our organizations and the people who work there, but that are not perceived in the same way by others. And so we need to examine how to address insecurity, not create it.

Just how do you go about alleviating insecurity and enhancing security? First, in order to build security you need to build trust, trust in you as an employer as well as an individual employee's trust in him- or herself (we will address trust building in detail in chapter 18). As a leader, you need to demonstrate through your actions that the employee will be in a safe place "no matter what." You need to emphasize security.

While building trust is essential, it is also a long-term strategy. In addition, in the immediate here and now of a change effort you must set out to diagnose the threats to others' sense of security. And the only way to do this is to ask. Unfortunately, part of the trouble with security issues is that they are frequently so deeply personal that workers will often lie or color the truth about them when you do ask. People will "dress up" the issues in some other form—"The change is not a good idea," "The change is too costly," or "The change has not been thought out enough"—when in reality what they want to say is "Will I lose my job?"

Consequently, you have to be careful to ask your questions about a person's sense of security in a nonthreatening, nonjudgmental fashion. And you need to read between the lines and intuit their real answer. You have to be careful to listen for the real answer. Remember, sometimes, as is our human nature, we tend to lie when we feel threatened; we seek to protect ourselves.

Once you've spent time ascertaining the various threats that may be present as a result of a proposed change, your next step is to talk about and examine these threats. Then you must strategize about how to address them. But—and this is important—you must first have earnest conversations about threats prior to doing anything about them. Why? Because when you make people part of the conversation, you can engage them in the "doing," that is, in creating possible resolutions to these threats.

The more you engage people in conversation, and ultimately in the doing, the more you move them from being on the "heels of their feet" to the "balls of their feet." Insecurity is a phenomenon of being on your heels. Action is a phenomenon of being on the balls of your feet. What do we mean? If you are standing on your heels, you are stuck, unable to spring forward and more likely to fall backward. However, when you are on the balls of your feet, you are poised, secure, ready for action. And the reality is, you can't be standing on the balls of your feet and resting on your heels at the same time. When you engage people, when they are involved in the action of doing, they can't simultaneously be involved in insecurity.

Let's take a look at a fairly broad example of this concept in play. Suppose the overall conditions of our national economy are such that they threaten the economic circumstances of various organizations. This can easily result in a sense of insecurity, both for the organization as a whole and for its individual members. Now, imagine the type of negative energy that could ensue if management began implementing multiple changes and cuts, without feedback or input. The end result would be to actually increase distrust and insecurity and consequently resistance to efforts that might otherwise prove to be beneficial. The snowball effect of this can be devastating and result in long-term consequences.

Consider what might happen instead if in our above scenario leaders brought people together to talk about the economic situation and gave them a safe venue to talk about their concerns. From there, imagine the energy that might be generated if they were invited to participate, perhaps through the brainstorming of possible strengths, solutions, changes, actions. Of course, as a leader you wouldn't stop there. No, you'd engage people further.

You'd create groups, assemble teams to work on various problems, addressing ideas from your brainstorming sessions, exploring their potential, perhaps even taking them all the way to implementation. Remember, when you are involved in action, it is far more difficult to be involved in insecurity at the same time.

Of course, as with all resistance factors we've discussed, we're not suggesting that security will be a factor in all change. But it might be. And when it is, you must work to enhance security if you wish to address the resistance that occurs from a sense of insecurity, whether real or perceived. To do this, you must first and foremost work to create an environment of trust. That is your long-term strategy.

Second, you must take the time to talk to people, to find out what their level of threat is—or isn't. If they aren't feeling threatened, you need take no further action to address this potential source of resistance. Remember, though, people aren't always truthful; you must learn to read between the lines. And finally, you need to engage people in action, because when you're on the balls of your feet, you can't be on your heels too!

Resistance Factor 7	Antidote
Insecurity	• Enhance Security through Participation
	• Trust Building

QUESTIONS TO BE ASKED BY THE CHANGE AGENT

Do you feel safe here?

Does the change make you think you may be without a job someday?

Are you needed now? After the change, will you be needed?

Are you willing to try a new job?

CHAPTER 10

Resistance Factor 8: Norm Incongruence

Jeff was a new principal at the school and was eager to try out his belief in shared decision making and teacher collaboration. This was his first elementary school and this was the first teachers' meeting he was presiding over. In the past teachers had sat in chairs in a row, theater style. He purposely placed in the room round tables with about six chairs around each table to facilitate discussion and sharing of ideas. When the teachers came in, they paused and looked in wonderment at the seating arrangement. They then went up to the tables and rearranged the chairs into rows. Jeff stopped them and said, "I purposely put you at small tables to facilitate discussion and shared decision making." To that one teacher replied, "We don't operate that way around here. We always sit in rows and the principal just tells us what we are to do." The teachers in concert nodded their heads in agreement. Then they sat down in rows and waited for the meeting to begin. Jeff knew that he had a long road to go before his belief became a reality.

Jeff was right. He had attacked one of the norms of the organization—sit in rows and listen to one-way communication—and his belief flew in the face of that norm. You can't bring about the change until you first change the norms of the culture. Norms are ways that people, implicitly or explicitly, behave in an organization. They are behavioral, not attitudinal. They act as the compelling glue of the organization. All organizations have norms and these norms may be productive or nonproductive. But they are present. Any change that confronts the established norms of the organization will fail, or at least meet heavy resistance, unless you first attack directly the norms of the organization.

Now how do you do this? These are eight steps in setting norms:

1. Identify the operating norms, both explicit and implicit.
2. Distinguish productive norms from nonproductive ones.
3. Define the norms you want as your operating principles.
4. Determine which norms must be explicit and which may be implicit.
5. Analyze the discrepancy between the real norms and the ideal ones.
6. Reach consensus on new norms (not more than eight to twelve).
7. Reinforce the new norms.
8. Review your norms. (Harvey and Drolet, 2004)

In fact, by following this process we have found that we can turn toxic organizations into productive ones. Norms are extremely powerful, and when supportive of the change, they can do much to bring about the change. Conversely, when they are opposed to the change, they can do much to defeat it. If norms are crossed in the change process then you must first go about norm setting.

In this case, Jeff has to attack the norm of members' blind obedience before he can implement shared decision making. The teachers had become comfortable with unproductive norms of not saying anything and thereby not accepting responsibility for any decisions. Jeff had to address this directly or shared decision making would never work. (If the reader wants more on norm setting, he or she should refer to *Building Teams, Building People* by Harvey and Drolet, 2004, chapter 3.) Whenever you hear the phrase "That's not how we do it around here," you know you have a problem with norms.

| *Resistance Factor 8* | *Antidote* |
| Norm Incongruence | Norm Setting |

QUESTIONS TO BE ASKED BY THE CHANGE AGENT

Does the change confront the norms of the organization?

CHAPTER 11

Resistance Factor 9: Boredom

Peg had been teaching for twenty-seven years. She taught fourth grade. She was tenured and had seniority at her school district. She had seen changes in curriculum come and go and knew that none of them mattered. Her test scores were low, but what could you expect from the kids she had now? They weren't very bright. She had another eight years before she could retire and dreamed of that day.

The principal had brought in a consultant to work with the teachers on direct instruction, but she didn't care. The kids knew the stuff or they didn't. Also, all the data that was presented was too complicated and defied understanding. She was daydreaming through the consultant's presentation. She only had twenty minutes to go.

Peg was in need of revitalization. She was bored with her job, perhaps even her life. The antidote for boredom is joy. She needs excitement in her job—a renewed passion for what she was doing and how she was doing it. Instead, she was experiencing extreme ennui. She wasn't stimulated about teaching, about her kids, about the curriculum. Her resistance factor is boredom. How are you going to change her?

The antidote for boredom is joy—a sense that the change is fun. You've heard about the old saw that goes "I want to jump on a bandwagon." It is a joyful response. You never heard anyone say, "I want to jump on a hearse." That is the opposite of joy. So figure out how to invest the change with joy—with fun, with passion. If something is important enough to change, then it is important enough for you to consider how you are going to inject joy into the process or the change itself.

I remember a company I was consulting with that had a break room filled with all kinds of food—junk food, healthy food, frozen food, snacks, and so on. You could be in the "break" room as long as you wanted and you could have as much food as you wanted. The only restriction was that as long as you stayed in the room you talked about business and new ideas that might improve operations. They were magnificently successful. They had loads of helpful ideas and much spirited discussions. I'm not suggesting that you have a "kegger" every Friday at work. But I am suggesting that you put some joy and fun into your discussions of change and your implementation of change.

Relative to joy is celebration. You can't celebrate too much. You need to celebrate the small steps you have in the change process. When I was on the city council, I was known as the King of Pins, Plaques, and Proclamations. We celebrated everything from sports team accomplishments to yard beautifications to employee above-the-duty feats to letters of commendation to the staff. We celebrated everything. And the recipients were highly appreciative and supportive. We invested their accomplishments and the changes with recognition and joy. In that way, we saw the work of our citizens and employees blossom. We handled the possible issue of boredom with celebration.

Related to boredom is complexity. When something is too complex, it defies understanding. It is too dense and unclear. In the face of complexity, we just shut down. What we don't understand, we ignore. What we ignore, we are bored by and move past it to something that is fun, that is joyful.

The antidote to complexity is simplicity. There is an old saying—you can start with simplicity and then move on to complexity, but you never go from complexity to simplicity. It is important to state the change in simple, straightforward language. I am wont to say that if your grandmother with an eighth-grade education wouldn't understand your verbiage, then you haven't said it simply enough. Also the more complexly you state something, the more it is open to different interpretations. State it simply and it can't be misunderstood.

Peg was the victim of both joylessness and complexity. She needed joy injected in the change and words needed to be simple. Or she needed to get out of the business of teaching. Left as she was, she would be a help to no one.

Resistance Factor 9	*Antidote*
Boredom	• Joy and Fun
	• Celebration
	• Simplicity

QUESTIONS TO BE ASKED BY THE CHANGE AGENT

Do you have passion for your work?

What brings you joy?

Do you see any joy in the change?

Is the change stated simply?

CHAPTER 12

Resistance Factor 10: Chaos

Dixon wondered why most of the other residents wanted the gates. He lived in a gated community of twenty-nine homes, but the gates were broken most of the time. They were left open, and few people complained about the unlocked condition. Rather than incurring a large expense to repair them, Dixon proposed that the gates be permanently open. He received a hailstorm of e-mails arguing for the preservation of the gates. The e-mails asserted the gates slowed traffic and kept other people out. But traffic had not measurably changed, and no one had complained about the gates being open for the past three months. They must be worried about something else, but for the life of him, he couldn't figure out what the real reason was. It was almost like they were reacting as if they were afraid of disorder. The gates seemed to provide a barrier against chaos.

Dixon had it exactly right. The gates provided a sense of control, a sense of order. The removal of the gates posed removing the barrier to chaos, to a lack of order. This is a minor example but a real one. Change that poses a challenge to tradition, to that which seemingly provides control, will be resisted.

In 2008, the two Democratic candidates for the U.S. presidency were a woman and a black man. To many this posed a real opportunity for breaking gender or ethnic barriers. To others this posed a challenge to the all white-male tradition of the U.S. presidency. What if a woman got elected? Could she handle the job? This fear was not real but a perceived attack on a traditional pattern. Similar things were said about electing a black man. Many were convinced that chaos would ensue. To have such a dramatic change occur was perceived as something that would completely transform their understanding of the institution of the U.S. presidency.

That is the difficulty with transformative change. It poses such a challenge to the traditional order of things that it is strongly resisted. Consider the continued, and arguably intensified, resistance to the idea of an African American man in the office of the U.S. presidency, even after his election.

The truth is, transformative change, implemented rapidly, rarely succeeds, in large part due to this resistance factor. It is generally far better to engage in transactional changes that may ultimately lead to a fundamental change in the system. One could even make the case that the election of Barack Obama was in fact just such a transactional change—one that has the potential to lead toward a more transformative change in our collective understanding of the institution of the U.S. presidency.

It is far better to stress how the change will bring fundamental continuity with principles, adhering to the values and spirit of the system. It may, indeed, be transformative, but you must sell the change as continuing the principles that you believe in. If you don't, you'll summon up visions of an organization "out of control" or "uncontrollable," and you'll have resistance to a heightened state.

Now, the reasons that people give may sound plausible, but they are really tapping into their feelings that things will be out of control. You have ferreted out the real reason people resist. It ultimately may not be this factor, but you have, once again, read between the lines and determined the real reason. Why do they resist? It might be due to a fear of chaos. It is important to bring out the perception that the change will bring control, bring order to disorder.

Resistance Factor 10	*Antidote*
Chaos	• Continuity with Principles
	• Perception of Control

QUESTIONS TO BE ASKED BY THE CHANGE AGENT

Do you think that the proposed change will bring on a chaotic situation?

CHAPTER 13

Resistance Factor 11: Superiority

Mr. Abbott was always harassing his workers about their messy worksta-
tions in the shop. He just hired Mike and after the first week of work, he
visited Mike's workstation. To his surprise Mike had a perfectly clean and
neat space. He called everyone together and proclaimed, "Look at Mike's
workstation. It's clean. Look at yours. They are messy. Why can't you be
more like Mike? Congratulations, Mike." With that, he walked away, with
the satisfaction that he showed his workers a good object lesson.

After another week he revisited Mike and found to his amazement that
Mike had a messy workstation! Where had he gone wrong? What did he
have to do to get the shop workers to maintain clean workstations? Mike
was a real disappointment to him.

Mike was not a disappointment. He was set up for failure by Mr. Abbott
and Mr. Abbott didn't even know it. (Alas, I have to say that this was a true
story.) After the boss said how superior Mike and his workstation were and
he left, all the other workers browbeat Mike. Why was he "brownnosing"
the boss? Was he trying to make the others look bad? Or was he just uncon-
scious? Whatever it was, they wanted him to change—and he did, because
of peer pressure. And the boss was surprised and disappointed. He shouldn't
have been. Whenever you point out the superiority of one individual or one
circumstance, you're dooming that individual to failure.

In workshops I give I often have one person stand up and then I extol
his virtues. "He's a perfect male. He has the perfect body type." To that
pronouncement I usually get catcalls or, at least, murmured dissent. "He
has too long of a nose" or "He's too fat" or "He's too skinny." Or the like.
The minute I stand someone up as superior the audience tears him down.

That happens with presidential candidates or employer of the year award winners. We resist anyone or anything that is described as superior.

I worked with a school many years ago. This was going to be a "technology school," long before they were popular. The district office announced that this new school was going to interview all teachers, so only the best teachers would teach here. And they did. They indeed picked very fine teachers. But all the other teachers, who were not picked, felt they suffered by comparison. As one remarked, "What am I, chopped liver?" So all the other teachers sabotaged the school and undermined the selected teachers. They did everything they could to make sure that this new school didn't work. And it never did. It was a case of being set up for failure by the district office. Their pronouncement was innocent enough, but the results were far from what they expected.

Superiority, either intentioned or unintended, leads to resistance.

The way around this blunder is threefold. First of all, you should rely on peer recognition if at all possible. You should reward peers for recognizing the accomplishments of others. You should provide a time for this at every public gathering or meeting. You should ask employees privately to recognize the accomplishments of others. You should "salt the mine."

Second, you could recognize multiple workers and emphasize what they have done to earn your praise. By having more than one or two targets of your recognition, you dilute others' intention of tearing them down.

Third, you should stress that the individual is doing different things that are effective or accomplishing the organization's goals. These actions are not superior, just different. You emphasize behaviors that are effective. Nothing else.

Resistance Factor 11	*Antidote*
Superiority	• Peer Recognition
	• Multiple Recognitions
	• Recognition of Behaviors that Are Effective

QUESTIONS TO BE ASKED BY THE CHANGE AGENT

Do you feel the changer is acting in a superior fashion?

Do you feel that you are inferior for not changing?

CHAPTER 14

Resistance Factor 12: Differential Knowledge

The team meeting had been called to decide which changes would be made to the course curriculum for the fall. Miriam arrived right on time and was surprised to find her colleagues already there. "Didn't we say two o'clock?" she asked. "Yes," replied her colleague, "but we ran into each other at lunch and decided to start early." A little while later, Miriam raised the question of total points per project. "Oh, we decided that last week. Didn't you get the e-mail? Don't worry, we've already made the change to the syllabus." The last straw hit when they moved on to video selections. Her colleagues began eagerly discussing their two favorites. "Wait a minute, I didn't receive copies of those," said Miriam. "Really?" said her colleague. "Well, trust me, they are great. So then it's settled, we'll use these two new videos and not the others." Miriam could feel her blood pressure begin to rise. Well, she thought, maybe they think we'll all use those videos and change the project points, but it was going to be one cold day around there before she would make those changes in her class!

We've all heard it said before: Knowledge is power. Shared information, whether among organizational staff overall, or team members in specific, represents some very important key values—inclusion and respect. Conversely, differential knowledge—the unequal or incomplete sharing of information, whether intentional or otherwise—creates an atmosphere of unequal power that can rapidly breed distrust, competition, AND, consequently, resistance. Bennis, Benne, and Chin (1985) go so far as to suggest it is possible to predict that a change will be resisted based upon the degree to which organizational groups possess little or incorrect knowledge about the change.

Think about it. Have you ever found yourself in a situation where everyone was referring to a meeting or a memo that you either hadn't attended or didn't receive? How did that make you feel? Anxious? Distrustful? On the lookout? Protective? Resistant? If the answer is yes, then you have encountered what Miriam was experiencing—differential knowledge—that source of resistance that stems from a lack of inclusion, a dearth of information sharing.

Now, we need to remember that humans, being the creatures that they are, aren't prone to making decisions based exclusively on data—that is, in a rational manner. In fact, that is NOT really even the issue of resistance when considering differential knowledge. The underlying issue is really one of inclusion. People want to feel informed, respected, "in the know."

It may seem obvious by now, but the simplest antidote to an unequal sharing of information is—yes, it's pretty basic, isn't it?—an *equal distribution of knowledge*. Here is the bottom line. If you want change to occur, you must ensure that the appropriate people (the changees in particular) have an adequate, equal knowledge of the changes being proposed.

Equal sharing of information translates into a sense of inclusion, consideration, and respect. This can take you a long way down the road to change. However, without this ever so basic courtesy, you are doomed to engender hurt feelings and resistance.

It is important to remember that information must be shared whether people need it or not to make a decision. It must be shared even if the sharer doesn't think you will use it. Remember, information is inclusion and power.

Resistance Factor 12	*Antidote*
Differential Knowledge	Equal Sharing of Information

QUESTIONS TO BE ASKED BY THE CHANGE AGENT

To what degree do you feel informed about the proposed change?

What is your level of understanding of the change?

How much information have you received about the proposed change?

Do you feel you have received it in a timely manner?

CHAPTER 15

Resistance Factor 13: Sudden Wholesale Change

Dillon cringed. Shelia had to be kidding. It was one thing to make a few trial changes to the program, to see how it worked, but all of a sudden, these massive changes? This was so not the right way to go. Dillon liked the youth ministry coordinator, but her plan to drop all of their current teen programs in favor of a completely new format for the spring term, just three short weeks away, was pure folly. It was too much and too soon. He was sure all of the other volunteers felt as he did. He was going to oppose the change to the program even if it meant going all the way to the pastor. After all, he was acting in the best interest of the youth program. What was wrong with continuing on with the tried and true anyway?

Sudden, wholesale change—it can be as massive as the No Child Left Behind Act of 2002, or as localized as the rapid replacement of an agency's entire accounting systems. What both have in common are the magnitude or scope of the change, the speed or rate of implementation, and the propensity to foster resistance. Shelia, the youth ministry coordinator, put herself in just this type of situation by trying to change all of the youth programs in one fell swoop. The result—Dillon's determination to resist.

One of the more frequent errors made by many change leaders stems from their attempt to implement too great a change too fast and too early in the process. Why? Because people generally tend to resist large, major, wholesale changes. Black and Gregersen (2002) illustrate this phenomenon beautifully, detailing how the faster a leader tries to force change, the more shock waves of resistance compact together, forming a massive barrier to success.

Not everyone likes to dive straight into the pool; it's too big of a shock to their system. Personally, I know I like to get my toes wet first.

It's that way for many people—they like to try things on for size, take a test drive, and see how it feels before they are ready for more. So what's a leader to do when they have big ideas and grand visions for a better future? The answer is gradualism. Do you recall our change principles from chapter 2? One of my favorites is principle 6: If you want lasting change, do it gradually.

Rather than engaging in sudden or complex change, or both, most people prefer to begin with baby steps. They need to see measured progress. We've said it before, and it's worth repeating: "success breeds success." Remember our reference to the "theory of small wins" in earlier chapters? Ensuring that people experience frequent, smaller, successful changes can bring you a long way toward achieving successful change. That is why gradualism works so well to address the natural and predictable resistance you are likely to encounter when attempting to bring about sweeping changes.

A companion to our friend gradualism is trialism, and while the terms can and often are used interchangeably, let me describe a slight variation in the shades of gray between the two ideas. Gradualism fits well with our understanding of small, incremental, transactional changes—ones carefully crafted to bring us successfully down the road to transformation. Trialism, as we are talking about it here, is about floating a trial balloon, test-driving a pilot project before bringing the idea up to scale. Let's look at an example.

I once worked with an early childhood agency that had several satellite programs ranging across a wide service area. Close to the beginning of the service year, the director decided to implement a large-scale reorganization of staffing responsibilities. The plan was put into effect at all sites, at the same time. It was too much all at once and many staff members resisted—both outright and under the cover of sniping and sabotage—and they won. Had the director applied trialism, the outcome could have looked very different.

Instead of pushing such a major change quickly and across the board, the director could have identified one location, discussed her plans with the site-based staff, and taken the change out for a test drive. Doing so would have reaped many potential benefits. For example, a pilot program would have allowed the director and staff to work as a team, identify the merits of the change, discover where the pitfalls were, and collaboratively determine how to fix them. As an added benefit, this approach could have piqued the interest and curiosity of other staff members. Instead, the staff and director struggled and bumped heads for many, many months and no one ever felt very excited about the change. What could have been a very beneficial and productive change never really got off the ground or achieved its full potential.

Our friend Shelia, the youth ministry coordinator, could also have benefited from a more gradual approach, and one that included a pilot program before launching into a replacement of all of their teen programs at one time. Dillon may have been less ill at ease, less resistant, and consequently more likely to support Shelia's efforts if they weren't coming at him all at once. However, while gradualism and trialism are indeed powerful strategies, there is an additional ingredient that can add to their potency—celebration and small wins. Beyond the power of taking baby steps, people need to celebrate their progress and successes along the way. The value of this strategy should never be overlooked.

Before we close this chapter on sudden wholesale change, we'd like to offer a word of caution regarding the use of gradualism. Odiorne (1981) extols us to be watchful, to be cognizant that sometimes appeals for gradualism and moderation, when made by the changees, can in reality be a delaying tactic.

Therefore, while gradualism may indeed be a viable strategy for addressing resistance to quickly implemented, wholesale change, leaders should always be sure to clearly examine from where the suggested strategy originates. Is it just a stalling tactic from those that favor the status quo? It is a fine line. You must make the judgment call.

Resistance Factor 13	*Antidote*
Sudden Wholesale Change	• Gradualism
	• Trialism
	• Celebrate Small Wins

QUESTIONS TO BE ASKED BY THE CHANGE AGENT

Do you feel overwhelmed by the size of change being proposed?

Do you have adequate time to adjust to the change?

Do you celebrate the small, successful steps toward making changes?

CHAPTER 16

Resistance Factor 14: Fear of Failure

Seth was seething. He had ordered the implementation of the new inventory procedures nearly two weeks ago. He was stunned to discover the store staff still using the old procedures. When he demanded an explanation from the shift supervisor, she offered up a lame excuse about how the floor workers were afraid to try the new procedures, just in case they didn't do it quite right. Well, he thought, I guess that really shouldn't surprise me. As far as he could tell, the whole lot of them were some of the most inept people on the planet. Whenever he asked them to do anything new, they typically flubbed it in some way, shape, or form. On top of that, he was forever having to chastise them over their inability to do even the most basic of things right. He wished he had a nickel for every time he'd had to say, "Come on, people, this isn't rocket science!" Ha, he'd be rich by now. It just didn't seem to make any difference how often he told them that he expected 100 percent perfection 100 percent of the time, or how often he admonished them; they just kept screwing up. Well, he thought, I guess it's time for another public "butt chewing." Maybe that would finally get them moving with the new inventory procedures—not that they'd get it right, but they darn well better get started!

Silly, silly Seth. He had no idea that he had become his company's own worst enemy when it came to implementing change. Someone should have told HIM that nothing promotes failure like failure AND that fear of failure inevitably leads to resistance.

It is an unfortunate and far too common occurrence in the workplace: managers prowling the floors, looking for and pointing out all the things people are doing wrong. The ugly truth is that when managers focus on failures, a climate of fear takes hold. Consider the effect such behavior is likely to have when leaders attempt to introduce change into such an environment. Over time, as noted by Odiorne (1981), the atmosphere becomes one fixated on and fearful of even the *mere possibility* that things might go wrong. When organizational members, from top-level managers to direct-line staff, begin to focus on the failures that *may* occur, rather than on the number of times things actually work well, they are left with an evolving resistance to change overall.

It's really not such a surprising phenomenon when you think about it. If I live in constant fear that my boss is lurking around the corner, waiting to pounce on me for something I didn't do correctly, no matter how small or inconsequential, how willing am I going to be to risk something new? Not very! This can have a devastating effect on an organization's innovative capabilities; after all, innovation requires risk taking—and an environment fearful of failure is hardly conducive to even tiny risks.

Fear of failure has another, equally "frightening" side—beyond the fear generated from thoughtless bosses castigating staff members for every small transgression. We must also be mindful of the effects of history, particularly ones filled with failed change efforts. When an organization is riddled by a history of failure due to past change efforts, people will instinctively begin to resist future change activities.

Imagine, if you will, your director strolling in to tomorrow's staff meeting with this announcement: "Now I know that for the last three years we've tried to start off the holiday fund-raising season with a community auction, and we just haven't been able to make it work. But don't worry; this year is going to be different. We're going to try it one more time, only this time we're going to put your team in charge. Don't let us down!" Doesn't that make you want to run right out and give it the old college try? Or does it make you want to start looking for new employment, rather than risk being the team that fails THIS year? Nothing tears a team apart more than failure. Of course you are going to resist such an assignment—it would be insane not to!

As with other sources of resistance, there is an antidote to the fear of failure. Yes, people resist the negative, but they respond to the positive, to success and affirmation. Rather than harping on what people aren't doing right, a manager can gain much ground by sowing the seeds of positive recognition.

When you regularly compliment employees for their efforts and attributes, they are more likely to gain a sense of potency and confidence. Additionally, if these same staff are exposed to consistent praise, they begin

praise

to trust your confidence in their abilities. While praise is not the only type of feedback a manager must provide employees, it is an important tool in building an environment that is conducive to change.

Finally, we must recognize two things: the value of ensuring prior experiences of successful change, as well as the importance of using past failures as positive opportunities for growth. Why? First, because working strategically to ensure successes, even little ones, builds employee confidence. Nothing brings more resistance than repeated failure experiences; "We've tried it before and it hasn't worked" is the death knell for any change. You must ensure small successes to ensure the overall success of the change effort.

Second, an organization that supports measured risk taking, while at the same time embracing an openness to learning from past mistakes, reduces the resistance that stems from a fear of the consequences of failure. Had Seth sought to bolster and applaud past staff efforts, rather than berate and ridicule their every action, they may have been more willing to at least attempt the changes in inventory procedures. Instead, they resisted; they were unwilling to even try, for fear of unleashing another of Seth's famous tirades.

Resistance Factor 14	*Antidote*
Fear of Failure	• Affirmation
	• Ensure Small Successes
	• Learning from Risk Taking

QUESTIONS TO BE ASKED BY THE CHANGE AGENT

How frequently do you receive positive recognition for your efforts and input?

What is your organization's track record with implementing past changes?

To what degree are you encouraged to learn from your mistakes versus being penalized for them?

CHAPTER 17

Resistance Factor 15:
Extremes of Organizational Structure

Hazel knew that a change was desperately needed but that it had no chance of happening. She sent the needed change to her boss, but by the time it worked its way up the organizational chain of command, it had no chance of mattering. The organization was just too bureaucratic for its own good. Also the rules and procedures for proposing a change were so codified and cumbersome that it would take years for any changes to happen. She had worked for the federal government, and even their procedures were less cumbersome than these. She would give up and wait for retirement. It was too bad—the change was a good idea, even if it did come from the assistant to the assistant to the assistant director of the department.

Hazel was right. The more centralized, stratified, and/or formalized a structure is, the less change will occur. But be careful if you have no formalization or stratification—change will also not happen.

Hage and Aiken's (1970) definitive work has looked at the relationship between organizational centralization, formalization, and stratification on the one hand—and productive, long-term change on the other. The relationship between change and each of these structural variables is not linear, but curvilinear. Take the variable of centralization, put it on a continuum from highly decentralized to highly centralized, and relate that continuum to change. You will see a regression line that looks something like figure 17.1.

At both ends of the centralization continuum you have low change. High centralization means dominant use of authoritative command and high *de*centralization yields high autonomy and modestly controlled chaos. Everybody does his own thing, and no one provides direction. This, too, makes change difficult.

Catch 22

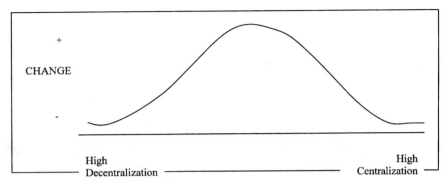

Figure 17.1. *Centralization and Change*

The greatest potential for change exists in the middle, where direction and participation are linked. Extreme organizational structures by their nature make resistance more likely and change more difficult. In other words, not only human but also structural variables give rise to resistance. It should be added that figure 17.1 could have been as easily drawn for formalization and stratification with the same regression line. Extremes of structure suppress the probability of change.

The antidote to this is simply to monitor your organization to determine if the structure is too stratified or formalized or centralized or if there is an absence of these variables at all. If your organizational structure is too imbalanced, toward one extreme or another, then you must first work with your structure to bring it to the middle. Not many organizations suffer from this source of resistance but those that do are in a mess. Without change there is only stagnation and eventual death.

Perhaps one of the most clear-cut examples of an extreme organizational structure would arguably be the Roman Catholic Church. To help us envision how resistance to change can play out in such a setting, let's look at a real-world situation.

Over the past decade, particularly within the United States, there has been a steady decline in the number of men entering the priesthood. The result has been a severe shortage of priests available to serve in their traditional leadership posts within local parishes. To address this situation several archdioceses and many parishes throughout the U.S. have been experimenting with a number of different parish leadership configurations.

One new arrangement entails a shared-decision-making model that includes a significant number of lay, or nonclerical, members of the parish community. A recent study (Broyles, 2007) of Los Angeles parishes that have adopted this particular type of shared leadership demonstrated a notable level of resistance to such a change. And, as might be expected, the greatest level of reported resistance emanated from those already serving in leadership roles.

The extremely hierarchical structure of the church has made the proposed change nearly impossible to implement or sustain at any significant level of long-term success. It was up against the "traditional rules and regulations" of the church. Heaven forbid, we couldn't change the rules.

Resistance Factor 15	*Antidote*
Extremes of	Moderate Centralization,
Organizational Structure	Formalization, Stratification

QUESTIONS TO BE ASKED BY THE CHANGE AGENT

Are the procedures and policies so formalized that not much change can occur?

Are there little or no procedures and policies in this organization?

Is there heavy bureaucratic structure in this organization?

Is this organizational structured so that no one reports to any one else?

Are there many layers of authority?

CHAPTER 18

Resistance Factor 16: Suspicion

George was suspicious of Jim's motives. He seemed to have a hidden agenda behind the changes. It might be a good idea, but he wasn't sure. He was plagued by nagging suspicions that Jim was doing this just to get himself some more favor from the "suits" upstairs. He wasn't sure the company really needed the change. He would take a lot more convincing and a lot more time to see if the change was good for all or just for Jim. He was certain, though, that Jim was not being honest, and that bothered him. He lived by the motto "when in doubt just stand there; don't do anything." He would adopt a wait-and-see attitude.

Suspicion. Suspicion. Suspicion, whether it be of a person or activity, is hard to overcome. It takes time and experience. It takes trust.

Trust is not a commodity unto itself. It's actually made up of five behaviors (Harvey and Drolet, 2004, 21–23). Let me explain each of these.

1. INTERDEPENDENCE

When I need you and you need me, we have a basis for trust. When I need you, but you do *not* need me, you can be arbitrary and capricious, and at some point probably will be. The adverse is equally true. Only when we have mutual need can trust evolve.

Think of the phrase spoken between couples, "You take me for granted." This is simply another way of saying that you do not demonstrate your need for me. A task sociogram is one way of assessing this condition in an organizational setting. Working with a group of five to ten, you ask everyone, "Who do you need to get your job done?" Then you look for mutual, two-way transactions—pairs of people who say they need each other. The more two-way transactions in a group, the higher the capacity for trust. The more one-way transactions, the lower the probabilities of trust. The more we need each other, both in reality and in perception, the more we can build trust.

2. CONSISTENCY

Research shows that people trust those who are consistent from word to deed and from deed to deed. Of these two, the former is most important—"I can count on you to do what you say." In a colloquial phrase, you "walk the talk." Much disillusionment with politicians reflects their inconsistency between word and deed. In the battle to win, politicians promise much; but in the face of reality, they deliver little. They talk about cutting back and then give themselves pay raises.

Contrast such politicians with one of our small-business clients, facing the recession of Christmas 1990. This businessman told his employees there would be reductions and cutbacks—and he started by cutting his own salary 25 percent and dropping all his club memberships. Those actions sent a message that he was serious and could be trusted to experience the same shortfalls as everyone else. Later, when business improved, he did not restore his benefits until everyone else's benefits were in place. He modeled what he asked of others. Other examples are university deans who talk of academic priorities and then teach regularly to show their commitment. Or elementary school principals who are regularly visible on the playground, at the bus stop, and in classrooms. Behavior needs to be consistent with verbal priorities. When you act in ways that say your words can be trusted, you enrich the entire climate of the organization.

3. HONESTY

People who lie, cheat, and double-deal are simply not trusted. You can get away with these behaviors in the short run, but in the long run duplicitous actions become widely known. You cannot hide this kind of light under a basket. Dishonesty can involve both commission and omission. Telling lies is not the only form of dishonesty; forgetting to mention the truth is also dishonest. When you are known to be honest and committed to integrity, you build trust.

4. AFFABILITY

Likable people are easier to trust. Affability supports trusting relationships. To be likable is not sufficient, however—although some leaders
foolishly try to build trust solely on that basis. The manager who walks
around being "one of the group" but is without substance may be well-
liked—but is not apt to be trusted on the professional level necessary to
build effective teams. Likewise, colleagues or managers who persistently
express negative attitudes and whine about everything are hard to relate
to. I worked for a university president who whined and moaned about all
the catastrophes about to befall us. In the process, he was trying to set
himself up as the university's savior. All he accomplished was to make
himself the least liked and least trusted person on campus. Affability,
though only fourth on this list, does still contribute to trusting, positive
relationships.

5. EXTENSION OF TRUST

There is an old but true aphorism that says, "Those who give trust, get
trust." When you send messages to colleagues that you will give trust only
when they "deserve" it, you set up cautious and untrusting relationships.
No, this is not a Pollyanna world in which everyone is loving and nice.
When you extend trust, you may well be violated. You need to anticipate
such eventualities and think through in your own mind what you will do
when they occur. But if you avoid extending trust for fear of violation,
you will then be a double victim—they will have achieved their purpose,
and you will have gained nothing at all. Your fear of giving trust will
make you a less trusted person. Remember, the messages you send are the
messages you receive—"those who give trust, get trust."

When these five conditions—interdependence, consistency, honesty,
affability, and extension of trust—are present, the soil is fertile for trust.
This equation is not perfectly predictive, but the probability is high that
when these five conditions exist, trust does also. With trust, you have a
richer organizational climate.

The antidote to suspicion is these five behaviors. To overcome George's
suspicion of Jim, Jim must first act in a manner that demonstrates interdependence, that Jim needs George and that George needs Jim, that George

needs the proposed change and the proposed change needs him. This is the first and foremost behavior that Jim needs to manifest. Then he needs to act in a consistent fashion, and it takes time to demonstrate consistency. Then Jim needs to be honest and convey his hidden agenda. Otherwise George won't trust him. Jim must also be a likable person and extend trust to George, though these qualities are far less important than the first three. In these ways, Jim will overcome George's resistance factor of suspicion.

It is through trust of the changer, and hence the change, that we can overcome the suspicion of hidden agendas and covert intentions. Without trust there is no change.

Resistance Factor 16	*Antidote*
Suspicion	Trust

QUESTIONS TO BE ASKED BY THE CHANGE AGENT

Are you suspicious of the change or changer? Why?

CHAPTER 19

Resistance Factor 17: Ambiguity

Clarence was completely confused. He had been listening to the presenta-
tion by the human resource department for more than half an hour and
he still couldn't figure out what in the world *they were talking about. It*
sounded like they were planning to make some sort of change to how em-
ployees could earn and use "comp" time, but for the life of him, Clarence
could not tell what it was they were really *expecting everyone to actually*
do. From the sound of it, he wasn't convinced they really knew either.
The HR director had already contradicted the payroll manager twice, and
the benefits coordinator wasn't helping at all. Every time she opened her
mouth, she used such complicated language Clarence was about to start
calling her the "human thesaurus." Were they going to earn more comp
time? Less? Not use it on Fridays? Who the heck knew! If they thought he
was going to do anything until they figured out what in the heck they were
even changing, they were on a different planet. He sighed, got up, and left
the meeting—what a colossal waste of time that had turned out to be. As
far as he was concerned, he was going to keep doing just exactly what he
had been doing all along, at least until HR got their act together enough to
say things in a way that was intelligible. In fact, he thought, I'm going to
go back to my office right now and complete my time sheet, and I'm going
to use my comp time just like I always have. I'm not going to be changing
a thing, no sir!

Ambiguity. Look it up in the dictionary, and you'll find it defined as a
sense of uncertainty, inexactness, something that is open to wide interpretation. This, unfortunately, is *exactly* what Clarence was up against. The
change being proposed by his HR department was clearly unclear—and
not just to the changees in the assemblage! There appeared to be an
equally distinct lack of agreement even among the so-called change

agents in our story. Alas, the end result was easily anticipated—*ambiguity inevitably leads to resistance.* Clarence left the meeting determined NOT to make any changes until someone could comprehensibly articulate just what in the world everyone was expected to do differently.

Within the context of the organizational change process, ambiguity tends to materialize as a result of two different but similar conditions. In the first situation, ambiguity arises when there is a lack of agreement about what is to be done and what changes are actually supposed to be made. This lack of agreement can occur between change agents, among changees, or both. When a proposed change is open to broad interpretation, people inherently resist moving forward—after all, how do you know where you are going if the direction isn't clear?

The second type of ambiguity is similar to the first, in that it involves confusion. However, in this case, ambiguity occurs because the changee does not understand the nature of the proposed change. This can be the result of confusing, ill-defined change proposals or change efforts that are too complex, and consequently difficult to comprehend all at once, or because the change agent has simply done a poor job of articulating what it is they hope to achieve. In these cases, some or all aspects of the change are confusing to the people who will be affected by or charged with the implementation of the expected changes.

You may be wondering how this is different from resistance that occurs as a result of differential knowledge. The difference is subtle, but clear. In the latter, resistance happens in response to an unequal sharing of information. People feel left out of the loop, uninformed. In the former, resistance occurs because the change itself is ambiguous or unclear.

These two forms of ambiguity are not mutually exclusive. They can, and often do, occur simultaneously, or one tends to follow the other. A lack of agreement among change leaders leads to confusion and poorly articulated change proposals. The end result, in both cases, is resistance. Fortunately, there are antidotes to ambiguity: clarity and simplicity. Let's briefly examine each.

First, let's look at *clarity.* In the case of a lack of agreement among change agents, an absence of clarity typically begins at the beginning— with problem definition. In other words, the ambiguity stems from a poorly or incompletely defined problem. You can't have a clear solution, or change, if you don't have agreement on what the problem is to begin with. There are many tools available to assist you with problem definition.

We suggest *The Practical Decision Maker* (Harvey, Bearley, and Corkrum, 2002) as a good place to start. A clearly articulated problem is your first step in a well-communicated solution.

That leads us to the second component of clarity—to avoid ambiguity you must not only know what solution or change you want to propose but also convey it so that others can understand you. That is why, and we can't emphasize this enough, it is critical for you speak in *plain English*! If you skirt around issues and use jargon fifty-cent words, people will not know what you want. And if people don't know what you want, they will resist doing anything. Know what you want to say, and say it so that others can understand you. It's that simple.

Speaking of simple, that's right, K.I.S.S.: keep it simple, s—. We'll let you fill in the last word to suit your own tastes, but that's the bottom line. People can grasp simplicity, but once we try to undertake complex or convoluted changes, we run the risk of creating ambiguity and confusion. Why? Because it can be much too much to digest at one time. That is why, throughout this book, we have continually emphasized the importance of taking baby steps.

That doesn't mean you can't or shouldn't implement complex change; you can, but you need to do so over a longer period of time, and your change must be tied to a clearly articulated vision. In other words, to achieve your vision, or to embark on a path to transformational change, you must start with a series of clear, simple, and unambiguous changes. Doing so will reduce resistance and build your chances of success all at the same time.

Resistance Factor 17	*Antidote*
Ambiguity	• Clarity
	• Simplicity

QUESTIONS TO BE ASKED BY THE CHANGE AGENT

Do you feel like the proposed change is described in clear, understandable language?

Is there clear agreement on what changes are to be made?

Do you see the change as simple and easy to comprehend or too complex to follow?

CHAPTER 20

Resistance Factor 18:
Lack of Leadership Skills

The entire room seemed to let out a collective groan, but Bob was, as usual, totally unaware. He just kept blathering on with his most recent PowerPoint detailing the "great new change" they were making to the lunch period schedules at all of the district middle schools. Slide after slide, he droned on and on. Mike leaned over and whispered to Tara, "Good grief! The man has the personality of Attila the Hun. He doesn't have a clue *what our lives are really like. When's the last time he's spent any time on* your *school campus? He hasn't been to mine in at least three months. To top it off, the man couldn't find his hat even if he had both hands on it!" Tara smiled. Ducking her head behind her notebook, she snickered and said in a low voice, "I know what you mean. It wouldn't be so bad if he had even* the slightest inkling *about what he was doing. You'd think he would at least have had the sense to ask someone for help with his presentation. But NO! Instead, he put this whole cockamamie thing together by himself. Look at it! A monkey could have done it better. Besides that, his whole plan for actually implementing his 'brave new schedule' makes about as much sense as jumping into a volcano. You know what? I'm NOT doing this! I don't care what he says. As a matter of fact, I know many of the other principals are feeling the same way and you should hear what the teachers in my building are saying! I'm going to fight this. What do you say? Are you in?"*

Bob doesn't know it yet—he's too unaware of his own surroundings—but his "great" change plans are about to hit a wall. The saddest thing is, he won't even know exactly why. He is on the road to an encounter with resistance—the type generated by his own lack of skills—both as a manager and as a change leader.

One of the causes of resistance that often goes overlooked, perhaps because of its source, is the resistance generated as a result of poor leadership skills. After all, if we are the ones leading a change effort, it can be easy—unfortunate but easy—to miss our own contribution to the emergence of resistance. What we fail to notice or recognize is that people often resist change because of issues with the change leader. Let's take a look at our scenario for some examples.

In the case of Bob, Mike, and Tara, we hear one of the principals in the audience describe Bob as having the personality of "Attila the Hun." I don't know about you, but I can certainly imagine how hard it would be to generate enthusiasm about a change—whether it had merit or not—if I felt negatively about the person proposing the new idea. And it doesn't have to be an overall personality trait, such as in Bob's case—this type of resistance can also stem from personality conflicts that originate between change leaders and changees.

For instance, while Mike might resist Bob's idea solely because of his perception of Bob's personality, another principal might actually find Bob's demeanor to be assertive and commanding. However, if Bob remains clueless about how others perceive him, he can unwittingly generate unnecessary resistance. Strong people skills are essential to good leadership—and this includes change leadership. Without knowledge of how people perceive you, and without the ability to connect with others, it is difficult to inspire enthusiasm in people when it comes to implementing change. Let's take a real-world example of this phenomenon.

I recall the efforts of a new director. Early in her tenure, she engaged in a 360-degree survey to discover how her staff perceived her skills as a leader. The intent of such an endeavor is to discover your strengths along with areas for growth. It also allows managers to check their own perceptions of themselves against how others see them. The director in this situation saw herself as very skilled and beloved, and expected that the staff saw her in the same way. Alas, this was not the case—the staff rated the director quite poorly. While this could have been a learning opportunity, sadly, it was not. The director's response was to dismiss the results and "chalk it up" to "proof" that the staff simply had "issues with authority." As a result, throughout the remainder of her time at this company she became more and more reliant on power-coercive change and management strategies.

As you will recall from chapter 1, such strategies increase resistance and sow the seeds of your ultimate downfall. Such was the case with this director. Her lack of leadership skills was her ultimate demise.

Now, let's delve a little further into our scenario and see what else we can discover. Did you hear Mike complaining that Bob rarely spent time at his school to see how things were going? It sounded like Tara felt the same way. What does that tell us? For one thing, it provides further evidence that Bob is lacking in the type of leadership skills that are crucial when it comes to implementing change. Why? To begin with, it has left the principals feeling that Bob is out of touch with their daily lives—he hasn't conveyed an understanding of what their needs and challenges are. He's not there, so how can he know? If he doesn't know, how can they trust him to propose changes that are going to be of any value to them?

We believe one of the things all good leaders must do is embrace the concept of MBWA—Management by Walking Around. Doing so keeps you in touch not only with what's going on in your organization—but also with the people who work for you. And that's worth more than its weight in gold!

Consider the benefits to such a leadership strategy. Your people know you, and they begin to develop a sense of trust in your interest in them. Additionally, if you display a genuine interest in others, staffers come to believe that you really do understand their needs. Consequently, when you propose a new idea, people are more likely to trust that you have everyone's best interests in mind, and as a result they may be more inclined to line up behind you. Unfortunately, Bob didn't get out to see his people in the field much. The result? They didn't trust his ability to know what they needed. That directly contributed to their sense of resistance.

Oh, if those had been Bob's only flaws! Sadly, there were at least a few more. Can you find them? That's right—he didn't ask anyone for help, even though he clearly didn't seem to be particularly familiar with how to organize lunch schedules. He definitely didn't seem to know much about how to facilitate a meeting either, and he certainly had a few things to learn about how to create an interesting presentation.

According to Waddell and Sohal (1998), inappropriate or poor management styles are one of four main social factors that can contribute to resistance in organizational settings. Considering this, it would seem fair to say that poor Bob was batting a thousand in his lack of both people skills and effective leadership skills. You might go so far as to even say he wasn't particularly savvy at being a leader. This lack of "savvyness" and skill all conspired against Bob, leading headlong into a brewing rebellion over his proposed changes to the lunch schedules.

There is a way out of this type of dilemma, where resistance arises out of a combination of poor people skills and inappropriate management and leadership practices. Naturally, a lack of skill can be countered by an intentional development of skill. This is not a quick-fix solution, nor is there one. It requires time and practice. In a manner of speaking, you, as a change leader, must "dig the well before you are thirsty." You must develop positive relationships, learn about and refine effective leadership styles and strategies, and finally, develop a solid understanding of how to match the most appropriate change processes with the environment in which you are working. Two excellent resources that we would recommend for information on the development of leadership skills and styles include DeLuca's (1998) *Politically Savvy: Systematic Approaches to Leadership Behind the Scenes*, and *The Politically Intelligent Leader*, by White, Harvey, and Kemper (2007).

Before we move on we'd like to add a note of distinction between resistance emanating from a lack of skills on the part of leadership and the concept of potency (i.e., believing you have the capability to make a change). While each is related to ability, in the first instance, we are talking about the abilities of the leader and how their skill, or lack thereof, can impede the effective facilitation of change. In the latter instance, we are referring to the level of ability the changee has, whether actual or perceived, to successfully make the change.

While the change leader can directly influence this latter situation, it is not the same source of resistance. This distinction is important in that it is essential for the change leader to be able to effectively diagnose potential sources of resistance in the change process. After all, if you cannot effectively diagnose, you are very unlikely to be able to utilize the positive aspects of resistance to their full capacity. Perhaps even more importantly, because this source of resistance typically emanates from a lack of skill on the part of the change leader, you as that leader must be aware of and willing to explore your own contributions to the presence of resistance.

| *Resistance Factor 18* | *Antidote* |
| Lack of Skill | Leadership Skills Development |

QUESTIONS TO BE ASKED BY THE CHANGE AGENT

Does the change agent have strong people skills?

CHAPTER 21

Resistance Factor 19: Inertia

Lily heard a lot of good things coming from the presidential challenger's mouth. She also heard the president say some good things. But the truth was, she didn't care. As far as she could tell, whoever was elected, they weren't really going to affect her life. She wasn't even sure she was going to vote. She thought to herself, "Why change a horse in midstream?" Besides, her vote didn't matter anyway. As long as she got three square meals a day and had a roof over her head, well, that was all that mattered. She was apathetic and proud of it. She'd watch a little more television, maybe a few sitcoms until bedtime, and then turn in. Tomorrow would be another day like any other day. "Oh well," she yawned as she flipped through the channels. She was content.

Why do so many incumbents get reelected, despite the low satisfaction ratings of politicians? Inertia. Most people stick with the status quo despite their intense dislikes for the current office holder. They prefer to just vote for the incumbent rather than examining who would serve their needs best. This is, in part, why incumbents have a huge edge.

Inertia. According to the laws of physics, inertia is the resistance of any given object to a change in its current state of motion. This state of motion could be nil—that is the object is at rest, sitting happily in place, or the object may be plugging along in some uniform motion, heading wherever it happens to be going. The degree of resistance an object has is directly proportional to the size of the object. In other words, the greater the mass of a particular object, the more inertia it possesses, and, consequently, the greater its resistance to change. Overcoming this inertia, or better yet, redirecting this motion, or lack of it, requires the application of a certain amount of energy by some external force.

The properties of inertia we've just described are not only applicable to objects; they can just as easily be applied to people. From this perspective inertia can be equated with inaction, a tendency to do nothing, a desire to stay the course.

Consider Lily from our opening story. Just like Lily, a preponderance of people tend to look at their lives and their circumstances and say to themselves, "I don't feel like . . ." You can fill in the blank. *I don't feel like dealing with the hassle of finding out about the other candidates. I don't feel like rocking the boat, risking the consequences of a new person's agenda. After all, the devil I know is better than the one I don't. I don't have the energy to move, and I just don't care. I'm content right where I am.* As long as this "feeling" of inertia exists, most people are not going to willingly opt for the change.

Thus far, we've talked about inertia in the context of the individual person, and while inertia can and definitely does manifest itself within a single individual, it is also frequently found within teams, and even entire organizations. In the latter two cases, such inertia is often deeply ingrained in the culture of either the team or the organization itself.

Culture encompasses those agreed-upon attitudes and behaviors of any given group. It includes our habits, our beliefs, and our most deeply held values. Culture gives us stability, perhaps even comfort. In addition, we are predisposed to resist anything that tries to move us away from our culture, and most assuredly from what is comfortable.

The more rigid we are in our beliefs and habits, the greater our resistance, our inertia. After all, our culture, by its very nature, acts to reinforce these ingrained behaviors and attitudes and to resist anything seen as outside our agreements with one another, to resist anything that threatens what is comfortable, known.

Additionally, as with our other principles of inertia, the size of the mass matters. The larger the number of team members, the greater the potential level of inertia, the higher the potential resistance. Extrapolate this to an entire organization, or even a community or national system, and you can imagine the exponential potential for resistance.

It is only with some sense of urgency that people will abandon inertia and seek to make different choices. Only where there is some stress in the system will people seek change. People who are content will stay that way. We'd like to believe that change is rational, and individuals choose change for considered and thoughtful reasons. But they don't. They need some stress or urgency to break the stranglehold of inertia. There is no simpler reason than that. No stress leads to no change. And it isn't just individuals, teams, or organizations that are the potential victims of inertia; oftentimes it can be a much larger system. Let's take an example from the pages of our own history book and explore the unfolding of the civil rights movement.

In the early years of our history as a nation, the practice of slavery was viewed as economically useful to the dominant culture, and consequently it was ardently maintained. We didn't change it, even though it was right and just to do so. It was only with the introduction of a sense of stress, a sense of urgency, that this practice was challenged. The anguish of the Civil War allowed Lincoln to free the slaves. When the pre–Civil War states of the North discovered that they were unable to viably compete with their southern counterparts, they began to argue for an end to slavery. As we know, a civil war ultimately ensued. It was this war that served as the stressor that spurred President Lincoln to issue perhaps what became his most famous set of executive orders, the Emancipation Proclamation. It also precipitated the eventual passage of our thirteenth amendment, officially abolishing slavery within the United States.

Of course, as we know, the thirteenth amendment, while immensely important, was only one step forward in the battle for civil rights for African Americans in the United States. It wasn't until World War II, marked by the U.S. Army's skyrocketing need for new recruits, that another significant stressor was introduced into the system. It was this palpable sense of urgency, this introduction of an additional stress, that led to a more focused, active, and urgent effort directed at recruiting African Americans into the ranks of the military.

While the circumstances of World War II and the needs of the military surely helped move forward our growing sense of not only the futility but also the moral reprehensibility of discriminating against people of color, it was not yet enough to effect more meaningful change. It took more. It took the civil rights movement of the 1960s, the March on Selma, the actions of the Freedom Riders, and the March on Washington to ultimately put enough stressors into the system to culminate in more transformational change. It was the introduction of a series of vital stressors, of hard-won transactional changes, that made it possible for the type of remarkable transformation that ultimately resulted in the election of an African American man to the office of the president of the United States, some 150 years after Lincoln's original actions.

Inertia. The reality is that some external force is required to initiate movement in a new direction. The application of enough force is needed to move the relative size of the mass one is trying to change. The greater the degree of inertia, the greater the need for stress.

But what of creating a sense of urgency, of introducing stress into a team, a system, an organization? In *Checklist for Change* (2001) Harvey addresses several strategies for change, including the use of authoritative command, sanctions, evaluation, targeting, and norm incongruence. Each has advantages and disadvantages, and the wise change leader must have the ability to select the strategy to fit the situation. Kotter (1996; 2008) too discusses the pitfalls of complacency and various strategies for generating urgency.

We encourage you to explore both resources. However, it is critical to understand that instilling a sense of urgency or introducing various levels of stress is rarely enough for change to occur. In the end, you must still attend to other resistance factors as well. For example, you will need to address people's belief in their capacity for change (i.e., their potency). You will also need to have a proactive vision of where you are going. The bottom line is that you will need a lot of things. But first and foremost, you will need a sense of urgency. Remember, without stress there is no change. When inertia is a dominant factor, you must identify and interject an appropriate level of force—in the form of urgency or some other level of stress—to induce movement toward change.

Resistance Factor 19	*Antidote*
Inertia	Stress

QUESTIONS TO BE ASKED BY THE CHANGE AGENT

Do you believe there is a need for this?

Would you just as soon stay with the status quo?

CHAPTER 22

Resistance Factor 20: Referent Power

Edith had a lot of misgivings about the proposed change. It might mean she would have to switch jobs or at least sales territories. She didn't welcome this at all. But Ed supported the change. He had never been wrong before. He was her mentor and, more than that, her friend. She implicitly trusted him. She had gone along with him on some other changes, and they had worked out well for the organization and for her. She would go ahead and do the change because she liked and trusted Ed. Oh, well, she would hold her nose and jump into the pool. Ed would teach her to swim.

From the definitive research done by French and Raven (1959), there are ten sources of power that still hold up in today's world. People that have power are:

1. needed
2. in control of resources
3. irreplaceable
4. close to decision makers
5. privy to information
6. able to create consensus and stability
7. interpersonally skillful
8. keepers of institutional memory
9. winners
10. trusted and liked by others.

who do you know operates off of Referent Power)

The tenth source of power is technically called referent power. Someone with referent power has the ability to influence others. They are often seen as people of character, integrity; people tend to trust them. They may even have a certain level of charisma. You respect them, perhaps feel a sense of affection, of loyalty, maybe even admiration. You go along with them because you can relate to them. You overcome your resistance to some*thing* because you trust some*one*.

This resistance strategy is different from the ones we've talked about so far. The other strategies started with a source of resistance that we then treated with antidotes. This, however, is an all-purpose strategy that you can use with any source of resistance. You may resist because of a perception of increased burdens, loneliness, insecurity, boredom, or whatever, but you're willing to go along with the change because you trust someone else. You like the other person and are willing to overcome your resistance on the basis of this friendship and trust. It's like learning to swim. You're scared to jump into the pool. You'll drown. But you do it anyway because you trust your dad. And, lo and behold, he teaches you to swim. You trusted him and he delivered. So too is it with referent power. You go along with the change, even though you may fear it, because you trust the other person. This is a strong strategy that trumps almost all sources of resistance.

So how do you go about making the best use of referent power? First, you must identify those individuals within your organization who not only support the change proposal, but who are also trusted by others. Once these individuals are clearly identified, you can strategically bring them aboard the change "wagon" and strategically use their support to garner the support of others.

One of the operative words in the sentence above is "strategic." This could mean asking trusted individuals to overtly support your change efforts, perhaps at a staff meeting or within their team gatherings. Or it might require more finesse and privacy, encouraging your trusted supporters to visit discreetly with selected individuals in face-to-face encounters. It is up to you to determine what would be the best strategy. But do be prudent in your use of referent power. While it may seem wise to convert resistors into drivers, and to use drivers (a.k.a. supporters) to move your change proposal forward, beware. If you create too many drivers, or if your drivers increase their force too much, or too quickly, you may actually end up increasing the very resistance you had hoped to decrease.

Up until now, we've talked about identifying others who might serve as a referent power. However, don't rule out your own ability to serve as a referent power. Of all the sources of power one may hold, this is the most potent.

Let's consider a few of the others described by French and Raven (1959). There is *expert* power, the kind you hold if you have unique knowledge or a specialized skill that someone else needs. However, being an expert can only take you so far, particularly when it comes to change. After all, just because you may know more about a particular change than someone else, or have specialized information clearly showing why it's needed, remember that human beings aren't necessarily rational. All the expertise in the world won't be enough power to inherently get others to change.

There is, of course, what we call *legitimate* power. This is the power of "authority," the power held by or bestowed upon a particular office or position. You recognize this power when you see it—it resides in official titles such as director, vice president, and captain, and in positions like police officer and principal. This power also has some definite limitations. For example, while people might "do what you say" because they have to, they might not be doing it because they like or respect you. Why does that matter? Ruling merely by dint of position has been proven to be ineffective time and again. Within the change arena this can be a real pitfall. Remember what we said about using push strategies and coercion? The more you push, the more you coerce because your authority gives you the power to do so, the more you are likely to increase resistance and stoke the fires of sabotage.

Beyond using push strategies, those in positions of authority have often been known to rule through their ability to control whatever resources are within their purview. Unfortunately for those who take this bent, they are only powerful for as long as the resources last, or they have control over them. I've known many a provost who has tried to rule either by dint of authority, control of resources, or both. Without exception, they were abysmal failures. However, I do recall one provost who used the power of his position in a far different way. He used his "authority" not to rule but to promote interdependence. He strove to build up others, to support them and nudge them toward their own personal and professional excellence. He demonstrated concern and caring, and he established trust. He developed his own referent power.

Referent power is indeed the most profound and deepest of all sources of power. As an organizational leader and change agent there is much you can do to develop such power and, consequently, influence.

Yukl (2002), in his work *Leadership in Organizations*, discusses various ways a leader might acquire and maintain referent power. He describes the importance of showing concern, acceptance, and positive regard for others; keeping promises; and performing unsolicited favors. It's essential to point out that these behaviors, if they come from a motivation grounded in manipulation, will ultimately elicit negative consequences. In the end, it is the demonstration of genuine caring that builds referent power, not calculation and aspiration for control.

We close this section with two final thoughts. First, as a leader and agent of change, it is not only important but also essential that you work at establishing your own trusting relationships with others within your organization and spheres of influence. For a more in-depth discussion about trust and developing trust, we refer you back to our chapter on suspicion—chapter 18. And finally, at least for now, suffice it to say that referent power, whether embodied by you or others, is an all-purpose strategy that can be used with any source of resistance, if you use it wisely.

Resistance Factor 20   *Antidote*
(Anything)   Referent Power (Strong Trust)

QUESTIONS TO BE ASKED BY THE CHANGE AGENT

Is the change supported by someone you really trust and like?

SURVEY

INTRODUCTION

Part III contains three separate sections, designed to support you in diagnosing specific sources of resistance that may exist in your organization as the result of a proposed change event.

The first section includes our survey instrument, which incorporates the various questions posed at the end of each of the chapters that describe our twenty sources of resistance.

The second section includes an assessment tool, which can be completed after you have surveyed various changees. An analysis of the collected survey responses can assist you in determining the degree to which various resistance factors may be present—ranging from "not at all" to "a great deal."

The third and final section in part III is a reference guide of the various resistance antidotes, arranged by resistance factors. Once you have surveyed changees and assessed the degree to which each resistance source may be present, you can use this matrix to help you strategize about the best ways to address and make the best use of any potential resistance.

One last word—remember to keep it simple. You can't do all things at once! We recommend focusing on no more than the two or three most significant sources of resistance as you move forward. This will help ensure a more manageable, more successful process.

CHAPTER 23

Questions to Be Asked by the Change Agent

You may use some or all of these questions to query participants about their source(s) of resistance to change. These questions correspond to the resistance factors described in chapters 3–22.

(1) Did you participate in crafting the change? If yes, how?

(2) To what degree do you think that the organizational leadership supports the change? Why or why not?

(3) In what ways do you see the new change as beneficial to you and the work you currently do?
In what ways might it add value?
What would you need to have so that the change provided you with more of a benefit?

(4) Do you get recognized for your contribution to this organization?
Does your organization celebrate your ideas and actions?
Do you have any participation in identifying or solving problems in your organization? How much?

(5) What does the change cost you in terms of (a) time, (b) money, (c) energy, and (d) skills?
What payoff can we give you in terms of (a) recognition, (b) achievement, (c) responsibility, (d) interpersonal relations, (e) facilities, (f) money, and (g) security?

(6) What is your current level of comfort and confidence with adopting this new change? Why?
Do you have an adequate role model to follow to implement the change?

Are you aware of others who have adopted this change? How do you feel about their situation?

(7) Do you feel safe here?

Does the change make you think you may be out of job someday?

Are you needed now? After the change, will you be needed?

Are you willing to try a new job?

(8) Does the change confront the norms of the organization?

(9) Do you have passion for your work?

What brings you joy?

Do you see any joy in the change?

Is the change stated simply?

(10) Do you think that the proposed change will bring on a chaotic situation?

(11) Do you feel the changer is acting in a superior fashion?

Do you feel that you are inferior for not changing?

(12) To what degree do you feel informed about the proposed change?

What is your level of understanding of the change?

How much information have you received about the proposed change? Do you feel you have received it in a timely manner?

(13) Do you feel overwhelmed by the size of the change being proposed?

Do you have adequate time to adjust to the change?

Do you celebrate the small, successful steps toward making changes?

(14) How frequently do you receive positive recognition for your efforts and input?

What is your organization's track record with implementing past changes?

To what degree are you encouraged to learn from your mistakes versus being penalized for them?

(15) Are the procedures and policies so formalized that not much change can occur?

Are there few or no procedures and policies in this organization?
Is there heavy bureaucratic structure in this organization?
Is this organization structured so that no one reports to anyone else?
Are there many layers of authority?

(16) Are you suspicious of the change or changers? Why?

(17) Do you feel like the proposed change is described in clear, understandable language?
Is there clear agreement on what changes are to be made?
Do you see the change as simple and easy to comprehend or too complex to follow?

(18) Does the change agent have strong people skills?

(19) Do you believe there is a need for this change?
Would you just as soon stay with the status quo?

(20) Is the change supported by someone you really trust and like?

Table 23.1.   Resistance Factors Assessment

To what degree do these resistance factors operate in your change efforts?

	Not at All		Somewhat		To a Great Degree
1. Lack of Ownership	1	2	3	4	5
2. Lack of Top Brass Support	1	2	3	4	5
3. Lack of Benefits	1	2	3	4	5
4. Lack of Recognition	1	2	3	4	5
5. Increased Burdens	1	2	3	4	5
6. Loneliness	1	2	3	4	5
7. Insecurity	1	2	3	4	5
8. Norm Incongruence	1	2	3	4	5
9. Boredom	1	2	3	4	5
10. Chaos	1	2	3	4	5
11. Superiority	1	2	3	4	5
12. Differential Knowledge	1	2	3	4	5
13. Sudden Wholesale Change	1	2	3	4	5
14. Fear of Failure	1	2	3	4	5
15. Extremes of Organizational Structure	1	2	3	4	5
16. Suspicion	1	2	3	4	5
17. Ambiguity	1	2	3	4	5
18. Leadership Skills	1	2	3	4	5
19. Inertia	1	2	3	4	5

Table 23.2.   Resistance Factors

Factor	Antidote
1. Lack of Ownership	~ Participation —in what?
	—how?
2. Lack of Top Brass Support	~ Top Brass Support
	~ Payoff for Top Brass
	~ Co-option of Trusted Advocates to Top Brass
3. Lack of Perceived Benefits	~ Meaningful Payoff
4. Lack of Recognition	~ Recognition Scorecard
	~ Celebration
	~ Participation
5. Increased Burdens	~ Payoffs
	~ Small Steps
6. Loneliness	~ Collegiality
	~ Change Teams
	~ Gradualism
7. Insecurity	~ Enhance Security through Participation
	~ Trust Building
8. Norm Incongruence	~ Norm Setting
9. Boredom	~ Joy and Fun
	~ Celebration
	~ Simplicity
10. Chaos	~ Continuity with Principles
	~ Perception of Control
11. Superiority	~ Peer Recognition
	~ Multiple Recognitions
	~ Recognition of Behaviors that are Effective
12. Differential Knowledge	~ Equal Sharing of Information
13. Sudden Wholesale Change	~ Gradualism
	~ Trialism
	~ Celebrate Small Wins
14. Fear of Failure	~ Affirmation
	~ Ensure Small Successes
	~ Learn from Risk Taking
15. Extremes of Organizational Structure	~ Moderate Centralization
	~ Moderate Formalization
	~ Moderate Stratification
16. Suspicion	~ Trust
17. Ambiguity	~ Clarity
	~ Simplicity
18. Leadership Skills	~ Leadership Skills Development
19. Inertia	~ Stress
20. (Anything)	~ Referent Power (Strong Trust)

Part IV

MODEL

CHAPTER 24

Resistance-Based Change Model

In this final chapter we want to pull all the other chapters together to form a resistance-based change model for your use. It has eight steps and is based on the change theory presented in chapter 2. It is transactional in nature and simple in its application. The eight steps are as follows:

1. Conduct a needs assessment.
2. Craft a needed change.
3. Float a trial balloon.
4. Assess resistance.
5. Develop a resistance-based change strategy.
6. Check the strategy against strain, potency, and valence.
7. Implement and institutionalize change.
8. Evaluate the change.

Each step is briefly described.

1. CONDUCT A NEEDS ASSESSMENT

Is there a need for change? You must do a careful analysis of your organization to determine what problems exist and what new ventures are called for. Both are important. You must ascertain what shortfalls exist between what is desired and what is happening. This discrepancy analysis serves to alert management to the problems that might be present. But equally important is the examination of what opportunities present themselves. What new ventures might you explore to capitalize on the new chances the changing environment provides? You need constantly to be watchful of both these circumstances—problems and new ventures.

2. CRAFT A NEEDED CHANGE

There are many ways to fashion a change in answer to your needs assessment. As a leader, you may come up with it yourself. After all, it is one responsibility of leadership to provide vision for the organization, and change requires vision. Another way is to have a small group, or skunkworks group, devise the change. The small group should be composed of leaders of the organization and people who are charged with the responsibility of carrying out the change. In that way there will be investment in implementing the decision.

A third way is to employ an open space technology meeting (Owen, 1997), in which a large group looks at the problems and opportunities of an organization and then selects which ones to work on. If you wish to pursue this, you may go to Owen (1997) to read more about it. Suffice it to say that this is a mechanism for getting a large group to consider change. However you do it, it is important to devise changes in response to a needs assessment.

3. FLOAT A TRIAL BALLOON

Once you have crafted a change, it is appropriate to issue a trial draft, to float a trial balloon. Why do this? It is simple. You don't want to paint yourself into a corner. If the reaction to your change is one of very strong resistance, then you always have room to alter the change. After all, it is only a draft proposal, not a final one.

You can try it out informally on a few people. Or you may issue a draft report. Or you can propose it for employee reaction. Or whatever. The important thing is that you always have the chance to revise or withdraw your change. You wait to give yourself the option.

4. ASSESS THE RESISTANCE

This step is the heart of our change model. After you've floated the trial balloon, you need to assess the sources of the resistance to the change. You do so by using our questionnaire in chapter 23. Not all the factors will be present. But at least one will. If there is no resistance, then the change would happen easily. But one or more will be present, because change always incurs some resistance on the part of some people.

You may use part of the questionnaire, because your instinct tells you what the source of the resistance might be, or you may use all of the questionnaire. You may ask people informally or you may ask a consultant to come into your organization and do a formal resistance assessment. However you do the assessment, you need to consider both the apparent and latent causes of resistance. You need to guard against your blind spots because your blind spots make you underestimate the intensity of the resistance. And that is definitely to be avoided.

5. DEVELOP A RESISTANCE-BASED CHANGE STRATEGY

After you've identified your sources of resistance, you develop your resistance-based change strategy based on the antidotes to those resistance factors. Now you can't address all the possible sources of resistance, so you pick out the three most salient resistance factors and devise a strategy.

For instance, the change calls for an alteration in bell schedule, and the three most important factors are lack of ownership, lack of recognition, and differential knowledge. Your strategy would be to form a committee composed of both supporters and resistors. You would give them a charge to come up with a different bell schedule that provides for x, y, and z. You would ask them to report back at each teachers' meeting and give them recognition for their efforts. You would have a party celebrating the final bell schedule. On their way to the decision you would also send the committee to other innovative schools to see how they handle the bell schedule. In these ways you would overcome their resistance and, thereby, the reluctance to change.

Whatever the factors are, you would: (1) assess the resistance factors, (2) determine the appropriate antidotes, and (3) craft the strategy. In that way you overcome their resistance and proceed on the road to change.

6. CHECK THE STRATEGY AGAINST STRAIN, POTENCY, AND VALENCE

Remember, change theory (chapter 2). We emphasize the principles of strain, potency, and valence. By that we mean:

- *strain*—in order for change to occur, there must be some stress behind the change, some urgency. Otherwise, we stay fat, dumb, and happy.

- *potency*—in order for change to occur, you must believe in your capacity for change. You must believe you can do it.
- *valence*—in order for change to occur, you need to have a vision of what you want to go toward, not what you want to get away from.

So you need to check your strategy for change to see if it has a sense of urgency behind it, but for the changee, not the changer. You need to check if the changees believe they can change, and you need to check for their vision of change. When these are in place and the antidotes to their resistance are provided for, they will change.

7. IMPLEMENT AND INSTITUTIONALIZE THE CHANGE

It is important to institutionalize the change before and while you implement it, not after you have implemented it. I have described in detail elsewhere (Harvey, 2001) the factors that lead toward institutionalization of change. You can go there if you want to know more about them. It suffices here to merely list the factors:

1. Preparation and Planning
2. Timing
3. Congruence with Mission
4. Environmental Sensitivity
5. Clear and Simple
6. Realism
7. Sufficient Resources
8. Central Leader
9. Reduced Proprietary Interests

Not all of these will be present in each change effort, but you have to attend to each, because four to six of them will make the difference between successful long-term implementation and only ephemeral change.

8. EVALUATE THE CHANGE

We often forget this step. We must gather data on whether the change is working or not. And beyond this gathering of data, we must use the findings to evaluate the effectiveness of the effort. Not every change works. You must see if it works and for which people and under what circumstances. Change left unevaluated is only voodoo.

This, then, is our change model. We suggest filling out the form that is presented in table 24.1. An example of a filled-out form is included as table 24.2.

CONCLUDING NOTE

This then is our resistance-based change model. By using generalized change theory, the resistance factors, and antidotes to resistance and then querying your changees, you can create change that has a high probability of happening. That is all you can ask for.

Table 24.1. Resistance-Based Change Model

Needs Assessment
Needed Change
Trial Balloon
Resistance Assessment
Strategy
Strain, Potency, Valence
Institutionalization
Evaluation

Table 24.2. Resistance-Based Change Model Example

Needs Assessment
—40 percent of the freshman are dropping out —Exit interviews point to irrelevancy of general education and financial aid as problems —The institution is 90 percent tuition dependent

Needed Change
—To have a new general education requirement that is both relevant to students and academically sound —Small committee of faculty, three students, and two administrators come up with a new general education requirement.

Trial Balloon
Try it out on faculty and students. Get reactions. Redesign it. Try it out again. Get reactions. Redesign again.

Resistance Assessment

Factors	Antidotes
Insecurity	Enhance Security
Increased Burdens	Small Steps
(Anything)	Referent Power

Strategy
—Emphasize that by making the curriculum more relevant we'll keep students and have more teachers and, hence, keep jobs. —Have somebody that is well liked and trusted by faculty on the committee —Implement the change in incremental steps

Strain, Potency, Valence
Strain—loss of students means cutbacks Potency—not a problem Valence—make the general education requirement academically sound.

Institutionalization

Evaluation
—Do exit interviews with students after the new curriculum is put in place. —Interview faculty on how the general education is proceeding —Check to see if attention is dropping

Epilogue

Now there lived in the land a hated king named Resistor II. He treated all his subjects with disdain and division. He was against anything that his subjects might suggest. He loved the status quo and was opposed to any changes. His subjects were highly displeased and wished for his ouster.

Then one day there rode into the kingdom a group of pilgrims called Antidocians. They saw how the king was hated, and they felt sorry for the kingdom's subjects. They started a great battle with the king. It waged on for years. Eventually the rebellious troops won and they overcame Resistor's forces. The pilgrims set up a government that was good and kind and thrived. The subjects were happy. Change was welcomed. All was good.

The moral of the story is that in time the Antidocians will overcome Resistors and change will be welcome. And it was good.

References

Bennis, Warren G., Kenneth D. Benne, and Robert Chin. *The Planning of Change*. Belmont, Calif.: Cengage Learning, 1985.

Black, J. S., and Hal B. Gregersen. *Leading Strategic Change: Breaking through the Brain Barrier*. Upper Saddle River, N.J.: Prentice Hall, 2002.

Broyles, Elizabeth Ann. *Resistance to Change in Conservative, Hierarchical, Religious Organizations: A Study of Roman Catholic Parishes Shifting From a Top-Down to a Shared Leadership Governance Model*. Ed.D. Dissertation, University of La Verne, 2007.

Clance, Pauline. *The Imposter Phenomenon*. New York: Bantam, 1986.

Collins, James. *Good to Great*. New York: Harper, 2001.

DeLuca, Joel. *Political Savvy*. Berwyn, Pa.: EBG Pub, 1999.

Fox, Shari. *Leading With Change Principles* (unpublished). Ed.D. Dissertation, University of La Verne, 2003.

French, J. R., and B. Raven. "The Bases of Social Power" in *Studies of Social Power*, ed. Darwin Cartwright. Ann Arbor, Mich.: Institute for Social Research, 1959.

Frohman, Mark. *An Empirical Study of a Model and Strategies for Planned Organizational Change* (unpublished). Dissertation, University of Michigan–Ann Arbor, 1970.

Fullan, Michael. *The New Meaning of Educational Change*. New York: Teachers College Press, 2007.

Glaser, John. *Leading Through Collaboration*. Thousand Oaks, CA: Corwin Press, 2005.

Hage, Jerald, and Michael Aiken. *Social Change in Complex Organizations*. New York: Random House, 1970.

Harvey, Thomas. *Checklist for Change*. Lanham, Md.: Scarecrow, 2001.

Harvey, Thomas, and Bonita Drolet. *Building Teams, Building People*. Lanham, Md.: Scarecrow, 2004.

Harvey, Thomas R., William L. Bearley, and Sharon M. Corkrum. *The Practical Decision Maker*. Lanham, Md.: Scarecrow Press, 2002.

Heifetz, Ronald, and Marty Linsky. *Leadership on the Line*. Boston: Harvard Business School Press, 2002.

Herzberg, Frederick, Bernard Mausner, and Barbara Snyderman. *The Motivation to Work*. New York: Wiley and Sons, 1959.

Hodgkinson, Harold. *Institutions in Transitions*. New York: McGraw Hill, 1971.

Kotter, John. *Leading Change*. Boston: Harvard Business School Press, 1996.

———. *A Sense of Urgency*. Boston: Harvard Business School Press, 2008.

Lewin, Kurt. *Field Theory in Social Sciences*. New York: Harper and Row, 1951.

Lippitt, Gordon, Peter Langseth, and Jack Mossop. *Implementing Organizational Change*. San Francisco: Jossey-Bass, 1985.

Lippitt, Ronald, Jeanne Watson, and Bruce Westly. *The Dynamics of Planning Change*. New York: Harcourt, 1958.

Maslow, Abraham. *Motivation and Personality*. New York: Harper and Row, 1970.

Mintzberg, H., and Quy Nguyen Huy. "The Rhythm of Change." *MIT Sloan Management Review* 44, no. 4 (Summer 2003): 79–84.

Odiorne, George. *The Change Resistors*. Englewood Cliffs, N.J.: Prentice-Hall, 1981.

Owen, Harrison. *Open Space Technology: A User's Guide*. San Francisco: Berrett-Koehler, 1997.

Pfeffer, Jeffrey, and Kathy Lammerding. *Power in Organizations*. Grand Rapids: Pitman, 1981.

Senge, Peter. *The Dance of Change*. New York: Doubleday, 1999.

Stinnett, Robert. *Day of Deceit: The Truth about FDR and Pearl Harbor*. New York: Touchstone, 2000.

Sullo, Robert. *Activating the Desire to Learn*. Alexandria, Va.: Association of Supervision and Curriculum Development, 2007.

Test, Elizabeth Ann. *Identification of Change Factors Influencing the Adoption and Routine Use of Institutional Technologies* (unpublished). Ed.D. Dissertation, University of La Verne, 1991.

Wadell, D., and A. S. Sohol. "Resistance: A Constructive Tool for Change Management." *Management Decisions* 36, no. 8 (1998): 543–48.

White, Patricia, Thomas Harvey, and Lawrence Kemper. *The Politically Intelligent Leader*. Lanham, Md.: Rowman & Littlefield, 2007.

Yukl, Gary A. *Leadership in Organizations*. Delhi, India: Pearson Education, 2002.

Zaltman, Gerald, et al. *Dynamic Educational Change*. New York: Free Press, 1977.

Index

About the Authors

Thomas R. Harvey is a professor of organizational leadership in the doctoral program at the University of La Verne, California. He has been the dean of the School of Organizational Management for fourteen years and is the author of several books, including *Checklist for Change*; *The Practical Decision Maker*; *Building Teams, Building People*; *The Soul of Leadership*; and *The Politically Intelligent Leader*. He was an elected La Verne city councilman for twenty-one years. He is currently the Abrahams Chair in Leadership Excellence, an endowed professorship chosen for excellence in the study of organizational leadership.

Elizabeth A. Broyles has been a consultant for nearly twenty years, providing a wide range of organizational development services to nonprofit, educational, religious, and government organizations. She currently serves as an adjunct faculty member for the College of Education and Organizational Leadership and the College of Business and Public Management at the University of La Verne.